D1458683

Bare beaches

The most beautiful way to be yourself

This book is dedicated to anyone who was born naked.

Written by
Mike Charles and Nick Mayhew-Smith
with Selina Gibbs

Senior artworker
Emete Isa

Printed and bound by
Slovart Print s.r.o.
Pekna cesta 6
834 03 Bratislava
Slovakia
www.slovartprint.sk

Produced under contract by
Wardour Communications Ltd

We welcome feedback from readers. Reports of suitable additional entries and updates on current listings are particularly welcome for inclusion in later editions. We thank you in advance for all such information.

info@lifestyle-press.co.uk

You can buy new copies online at: www.barebeaches.com
Or send a cheque with your name and address (UK only) for £14.95 (includes £2 post and packing) to:
Lifestyle Press
Wardour Communications
20-22 Great Titchfield Street
London W1W 8BE
Above details valid to June 2006.

Cover picture: The Bahamas

First published in June 2004 by Lifestyle Press Ltd
PO Box 1087, Bristol BS48 3YD

info@lifestyle-press.co.uk

www.barebeaches.com

Copyright © Lifestyle Press Ltd 2004

British Library Cataloguing-in Publication Data. A catalogue record for this book is available from the British Library.

Although the publisher of this book has made every effort to ensure that the information was correct at the time of going to press, the publisher does not assume and hereby disclaims any liability to any party for any loss or damage caused by errors, omissions or misleading information. The nature of the guide is such that the accuracy of the content may quickly become outdated.

We would like to thank the many organisations and people who have helped and encouraged the production of this book.

ISBN 0-9544767-1-9

Ever wanted to lie in the sun wearing nothing but your birthday suit? To swim naked in a warm sea? To drop all your stress and forget about your worries? To get a brown bottom?

If so you're in good company. A growing number of us have had the glorious experience of stepping out of a swimming costume for the first time and realising that it feels wonderful – and that best of all it's no big deal.

Not just a small number of us but a vast number. Millions. In fact roughly 10 million Britons alone have gone skinny dipping, and more than 5 million of us have sunbathed in the nude.

So you want to know where you can do it? Bare Beaches is the book your pale bits have been waiting for.

South Africa 188-189

Best bares

Our top five most beautiful, most family-friendly, best for a short
break, most secluded and most accessible **118-119**
Top five best for winter sun, best snorkelling, most romantic, most
popular and best mix of bare and clothed bathers **150-151**

Bare facts

Who goes bare?

Millions of people go nude sunbathing each year – but there's a first time for every bare bather. It's lovely to dream about going naked in the sunny outdoors, and if you dream enough, curiosity will eventually get the better of you. We asked some new and experienced skinny dippers what it feels like to go bare for the first time

Emma, 31, from London, tells her story. "I worked with someone who sunbathes in the nude and who kept telling me how wonderful it was. I couldn't quite understand his enthusiasm but decided that the only way to find out for sure was to **give it a go myself** and I have to say, I totally agree.

"I thought it would feel odd to be naked in front of other people, but it just felt so normal and friendly. When you are naked with other people naked around you, you almost share a vulnerability where **your guard is completely down** and it just seems so natural to be friendly and to talk."

Sue, 56, agrees. "When you are without your clothes, it **takes away all social standing**. You just feel so much more relaxed. It is like going back to basics and it is such a wonderful feeling. You just find you automatically get talking to others on the beach around you."

Sue had her first experience of naked sunbathing back in the 70s and says she hasn't looked back since.

"I remember the first time and it feeling so incredibly comfortable and wondering why I hadn't tried it earlier and

Picture left: Nicole Lejeune,
Maison de la France
(uk.franceguide.com)

7

what all the fuss was about." Sue now runs a travel firm specialising in nude beach holidays, France 4 Naturisme.

While it often seems **easier for women** to embrace this truly natural way of sunbathing, men are keen to join in. Mike, 31, recalls his first experience of going nude in Spain.

"I was on holiday with my girlfriend and we discovered there was a beach nearby where you could sunbathe in the nude and just thought, **why not?**

"At first, I must admit it felt very different to be lying on sunbeds with nothing on but **it was also very liberating**. We quickly realised that no one else around you cares about you being naked. In fact, I found the whole experience very relaxing and I'd **definitely do it again**."

Many people find their first experience of sunbathing in the nude an unforgettable day.

Gemma, 27, from Oxford, says: "I won't forget how wonderful it felt. I was with my sister when we were driving in Majorca and spotted a deserted beach.

"We initially went there to have a walk but afterwards we wanted to swim but realised we didn't have our costumes with us. So we thought **why not throw off our clothes** altogether and go for a skinny dip instead.

"When we came out of the sea, we lay in the sun to dry off. In the end, we spent a wonderful morning in pure seclusion, feeling the **sun on our bottoms**. It was a great experience and I'd definitely do it again."

French pictures (this page, below left; opposite page, top right, centre left, bottom right) Nicole Lejeune, Maison de la France
Portugal pictures (opposite page, centre right, bottom left) Quinta da Horta www.naturist-holidays-portugal.com

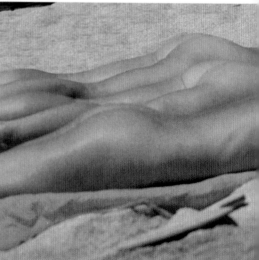

How to use Bare Beaches

Get your barings

Bare beaches, by their nature, are often in secluded and peaceful locations. It's what makes them so special, and in a few cases it also makes them harder to find. Most beaches listed in this guide have country or island maps indicating their approximate location. Use these alongside your own tourist maps to pinpoint exactly where you can bare and how to get there. We have also given directions to each beach. Don't be afraid to ask for information locally if you need help, tourist offices and hotels are well used to pointing bare bathers in the right direction.

Photography

Respecting people's privacy is central to the bare beach experience. We have edited all our pictures to ensure that all general beach users are unrecognisable. And yes, there are a lot of bare bottoms in the book. This is not only out of courtesy to beachgoers. On a bare beach, other bathers don't feel remotely in your face. It is a place where bodies are just bodies. Nothing is put under a spotlight just as nothing is hidden from sight. And while publicity pictures focus on the beautiful, absolutely anybody, of any age, shape, colour and size, is able to enjoy being bare on a beach. We would love to include more images in our next edition and welcome contributions. See the page opposite for contact information.

Before you bare

The popularity of bare beaches has risen relentlessly over the past few decades. But where discerning nudes lead the clothed masses may follow: this year's bare bathing heaven might be next year's tourist trap. We have made every effort to ensure the beaches in this book are well established for naked use. Many are officially approved for bare bathing, many have been used naked for decades and some are used regularly but without legal approval. If in doubt about whether you can strip, see what other beach users are doing, or ask at a local tourist office. For resort beaches listed in this book simply confirm bare bathing facilities when you book. Bare bathing is a largely unremarkable activity in most countries in this guide. Relax, strip off and enjoy to your heart's content.

Newer and nuder

We are publishing full updates to this guide on our website www.barebeaches.com. And above all we are including your feedback. So if you find that a hotel has expanded its bare bathing facilities, a beach has been over-run by clothed hordes, or you know another place we should list, please get in touch with us either by email:
info@lifestyle-press.co.uk
Or write to: Lifestyle Press
Wardour Communications
20-22 Great Titchfield Street
London W1W 8BE

France

No country has embraced the bare
beach experience more wholeheartedly
than France. Hundreds of beautiful
beaches, such as **Hatainville Plage**
on the Cherbourg peninsula (right), can
be enjoyed without a stitch of clothing

France

Bare bathing is deeply embedded in French culture. Every year millions of us are drawn by the chance to bathe naked on the country's coast. Unsurprisingly, the tourist industry has spotted this one and there are some fabulous resorts built around naked bathing. Yet more visitors simply turn up and get on with their bare beach holidays independently.

The south-west coast is almost one long, stunning bare beach, stretching more than 100 miles from the Gironde to Biarritz. There are a few bits of beach where you need to wear clothes, mainly around the towns. Cycle paths through the extensive pine forests make it easy to find the perfect sunny beach for baring your bottom in absolute solitude.

For a more sophisticated flavour, the sparkling Mediterranean has lots of sandy nude beaches. Cap d'Agde, the world-famous naked city, is basically a seaside town without the clothes. Other options range from stripping off within sight of St Tropez to walking through the empty flat beaches of the western coastline.

We've listed some of France's best bare beaches but if you're looking for one nearer your holiday destination, there are loads more. If your French is OK, this website has around 80 beaches – membres.lycos.fr/ucn/plages.html

Atlantic Beaches

Berck Plage

Berck sur Mer, south of Le Touquet

This wonderful wide sandy bare beach has lots of space. It's easy to find your own private spot for a truly back to nature rest. Backed by attractive dunes covered in **wild flowers and marram grass**, the French authorities have declared the shore an official nude beach.

Don't be surprised to see evidence of recent history by way of **World War II fortifications**. It's very handy for the channel ports making it ideal for a weekend trip from the UK.

From **Berck sur Mer** drive north towards **Bellvue** on the outskirts of town. Pass the **Thalassotherapy Hospital** and shortly you will see a car park. Walk on to the beach and turn right (north) – a **large sign** indicates when you've arrived at the bare beach. There is a bar, restaurant and shop near the car park.

Local information is available from the internet at: www.district-berck-sur-mer.com

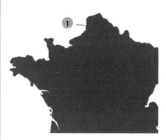

① Berck Plage

One of the nearest French bare beaches to the UK, **Berck Plage** has plenty of space to indulge in a bit of bathing free from everything.
Picture: Suzanne Piper

Merville Plage naturiste

Merville Franceville, 15 kms north-east of Caen
An attractive official bare beach of light yellow sand, east of the mouth of the **river Orme**. Ideal for watching the ferries from Portsmouth arrive and depart.

From **Merville Franceville Plage** take the D514 coast road west for 1 km. A lane going north leads to a car park at the nautical base, then it's a short walk to the bare beach. More info available from perso.wanadoo.fr/normand/site.htm

Hatainville Plage

Carteret, western Cherbourg peninsula
Sometimes referred to as Les Moitiers d'Allonne, this lovely quiet and unspoilt bare beach with **miles of golden sand** is backed by rolling dunes. The sea goes out a long way here, making it a pleasant stroll in the buff to go for a dip (see picture on page 13). However, beware of **strong currents**, as there are no lifeguards.

Travelling south from **Cherbourg** on the main D904, turn right on to the D242 to **Hatainville**. Go through the village and

it's 2 kms to the coast at Les Moitiers. Park and walk south along the beach in the direction of Carteret. Tourist info from www.barneville-carteret.net

St Germain sur Ay, à la pointe du Banc

Near Lessay, on the western Cherbourg peninsula
Acres and acres of **wild unspoilt bare beach** just waiting to be discovered. The whole shore is flat and the sea goes out a long way. Shellfish, shrimps and oysters can be found in the rock pools. Miles of **walking in the buff** to enjoy on this official nude beach.

Drive south from **Cherbourg** for 50 kms, first on the D904 and then the D650. Just before entering **St Germain sur Ay**, turn right on to the D306 to **St Germain Plage**. Drive as far south as possible and then walk in the same direction from the car park. More information about the beach is available from perso.wanadoo.fr/normand/site.htm

Plage des Chevrets, Ille et Vilaine

La Guimorais – St Coulomb, 10 kms east of St Malo
This bare beach is in an area of **picturesque coastline** and has a fine sandy shore.

Travel east from **St Malo** on the D201 coast road for approximately 10 kms in the direction of **Pointe du Meinga**. Park near the Pointe and it is a 10-minute walk to the **La Guimorais** nude beach, on the north-west side of the bay.

Plage de Kerminihy

Erdeven, south-west Brittany
A remote but pleasant official nude beach of gently sloping

Surf's up: Many bare beaches on the Atlantic coast have lifeguards, who look out for bathers in a controlled zone often marked by blue flags (see right, at **Euronat** resort's beach). But many more are unpatrolled and require care with the waves and tides

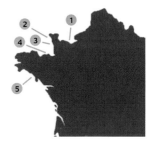

1 Merville Plage
2 Hatainville Plage
3 St Germain sur Ay
4 Plage des Chevrets
5 Plage de Kerminihy

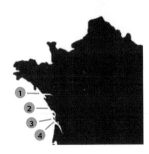

1 **La Turballe Pen Bron Plage**
2 **Le Petit Pont, Brétignolles**
3 **La Grande Plage, Ile d'Oleron**
4 **La Cote Sauvage**

La Pinede
www.ot-erdeven.fr
(naturist campsite listed)
Tel: 00 33 297 55 61 55

Cap Natur
www.cap-natur.com
info@cap-natur.com
Tel: 00 33 251 60 11 66
Fax: 00 33 251 60 17 48
Book through France 4 Naturisme
(Suzanne Piper)

sand and shingle stretching 2 kms north to the mouth of the Etel river. Easy access makes this beach a **popular spot for families**, especially as the resorts of **Carnac** and **Quiberon** are not far away.

Travelling north from Carnac on the D781 turn left in the village of Erdeven, signposted for **Kerouriec Plage**. There is a car park not far from the sea – walk to the beach and turn right for the Kerminihy bare area. Kerouriec beach itself is to the left.

In addition to lots of ordinary campsites and holiday homes in the area, there is a simple naturist site, **La Pinede (Centre Naturiste Bretagne Sud)** near Erdeven, 6 kms inland from the beach. Take your own tent, campervan or caravan. Tourist info is available from www.ot-erdeven.fr where the bare beach and naturist campsite are listed.

La Turballe Pen Bron Plage

La Turballe, near La Baule
A lovely long **undeveloped peninsula** backed by pine tree-clad dunes on the Atlantic coast, near the mouth of the **Loire**. The fine yellow sand and larger resorts nearby make this a particularly popular official nude beach, used by locals and holidaymakers alike. The variety of seabirds makes it a favourite with **ornithologists**.

Travel north-west from **La Baule** to **Guerande** then take the D99 to **La Turballe**. Go south on the D92 past the 'Village Vacances Famille' following signs to **Pen Bron Hospital**. In summer the road is gated and requires a pleasant 10-minute walk through the dunes to the beach. Tourist info from otsi.la.turballe.free.fr

Le Petit Pont, Brétignolles

Between St Gilles-Croix-de-Vie and Les Sables d'Olonne
With over 1 km of sandy bare beach to enjoy there is space for everybody on this beautiful coastline. Completely unspoilt, the dunes behind the beach are covered with **wild flowers** and **marram grass**. The nude area is between two natural outcrops of rock. Take care when swimming due to the **strong tidal currents**.

Drive south from **St Gilles** on the D38 for 8 kms. Turn right on to a track by l'Auberge du Petit Pont, at **La Sanzaie**, on the outskirts of Brétignolles sur Mer. Park at the beach.

In addition to a good choice of ordinary holiday accommodation there is a modern naturist resort, **Cap Natur**, 11 kms from the bare beach. Set in attractive pinewoods, it has apartments and mobile homes to rent as well as places for tents and caravans. Complete with both **indoor and outdoor swimming pools**. Tourist information is available from www.bretignolles-sur-mer.com

La Grande Plage, Ile d'Oleron

St Trojan-les-Bains, Ile d'Oleron

A fabulous open white-sand beach with acres of space and a completely **relaxed atmosphere** – swimsuited and bare bathers enjoy the peaceful setting in harmony. During fine weather it feels more like the Mediterranean than the Atlantic and the quality of the light attracts **artists** from all over the country.

France's Atlantic coast is far less developed than the Mediterranean, but with huge beaches and a clean sea it has become a favourite of discerning bare bathers

Take the impressive free **road bridge** on to the island (D26). At the end of the bridge continue 2 kms, then turn left, signposted **St Trojan-les-Bains**. On the edge of the town turn right, on to the minor D126 to the beach. Walk a few metres south (left) from the car park to the bare area. Tourist info from www.oleron.org

La Cote Sauvage

La Tremblade, between Ile d'Oleron and Royan

As the name suggests, this is a **wild and remote** beach, stretching over 12 kms in total. It is ideal for undisturbed sunbathing and for bracing long naked walks along the shoreline.

It's a beautiful place, but also exposed to the full force of the Atlantic swell. So with no lifeguards, great care is needed in the sea – signs indicate that there should be **no swimming**. There is a bar and restaurant at the northern end of the bare beach, by the Pointe Espagnole.

From **La Tremblade** head firstly north-west on the D25, through **Ronce-les-Bains** and into the forest. The road then turns south following the line of the coast. There are a number of car parks in the woods. Take one of the paths through the dunes to the beach.

The nude area is from **Pointe Espagnole**, south for a full 5 kms.

La Grande Cote

Between La Palmyre and St Palais, near Royan

Not far from La Cote Sauvage, this attractive sandy beach is popular with families because it is more sheltered and has easy access. Acres of **fine light golden sand** slope gently towards the sea, making it good for skinny-dipping in calm weather. There is a **sandwich bar** serving refreshments on this official bare beach.

Travelling south west from **La Palmyre** on the D25 towards **St Palais**, there is a car park in the woods on the left, 1 km past the zoo. Take the pedestrian underpass and a pleasant walk through the trees to the nude beach. Tourist info from www.la-palmyre-les-mathes.com

Euronat – Montalivet north

Montalivet-les-Bains, north-west of Bordeaux

There is a glorious expanse of **clean golden sand** in front of the Euronat naturist resort. The sea shore is open to the public and bare beachbums will feel especially comfortable in the company of so many like-minded souls bathing in the buff. However,

Euronat
www.euronat.fr
info@euronat.fr
Tel: 00 33 556 09 33 33
Fax: 00 33 556 09 30 27
Book through France 4 Naturisme
(Suzanne Piper), Peng Travel

there's plenty of room to find your own space. **Lifeguards** supervise a section of the beach for swimming and surfing. Popular with families and attracting thousands of happy holidaymakers at peak times of the year.

From the small seaside town of **Montalivet-les-Bains**, drive north on the D102 coast road. After 3 kms the road turns sharply right, inland. Park and walk on to the beach – the main bare area is to the right.

The well-known naturist resort of **Euronat** is large and modern, offering camping, caravanning and luxury self-catering chalets. There are shops, restaurants, a big indoor pool and even a **thalossotherapy centre** for **spa and seawater treatments**, all set in an extensive pine forest. It's a peaceful place much loved by visitors for its friendly atmosphere and an easy introduction to **nudist camping** (see page 44).

1 La Grande Cote
2 Euronat
3 CHM Montalivet

CHM – Montalivet south

Montalivet-les-Bains, north-west of Bordeaux
Another huge nude beach backed by dunes and pine trees, offering long bare walks and lots of **personal space**. There is a lifeguard and some great waves for surfing. Directly behind the

① La Jenny

CHM Montalivet
www.chm-montalivet.com
infos@chm-montalivet.com
Tel: 00 33 556 73 26 70
Fax: 00 33 556 09 32 15
Book direct

La Jenny
www.lajenny.fr
info@lajenny.fr
Tel: 00 33 556 26 56 90
Fax: 00 33 556 26 56 51
Book through France 4 Naturisme
(Suzanne Piper), Peng Travel

La Jenny, pictured below and on facing page, is easy to reach by hire car from Bordeaux airport, making it accessible for a mini-break without clothes. All pictures courtesy La Jenny

beach is the **naturist resort** of CHM Montalivet – the first purpose built nude holiday centre in France, which opened in 1950. It's still just as popular today, and although updated there's a definite touch of 'shabby chic' adding to the nostalgia. General tourist info from www.ot-vendays-montalivet.fr and www.montalivet-info.com

The beach can be accessed by parking in **Montalivet-les-Bains** and walking south along the sand to the bare area.

CHM Montalivet Vacances Naturistes offers acres of camping and caravanning space as well as timber chalets for hire where you don't have to wear anything. There is a large outdoor swimming pool and lots of sports available. Shops and restaurants on site.

Le Porge Ocean – La Jenny

Due west of Bordeaux

On the same long stretch of beautifully unspoilt coast as Montalivet, but 50 kms further south. This is the home of the peaceful and friendly **La Jenny** naturist resort, set in pinewoods behind the shore. The beach is in a remote spot with no towns nearby, so the bare area stretches for miles in each direction. There's no difficulty finding your own privacy here – it's **a place to escape**.

Travel west from **Bordeaux** on the D107 via Le Temple/Le Porge, then follow the direction of **Lège Cap Ferret/Arès** on the D3 to La Jenny. The resort is also well signposted along the way.

There is a lovely smooth **cycle track** running through the woods along the coast (no cars allowed) from Lacanau in the north all the way to Cap Ferret in the south, so it's easy to find

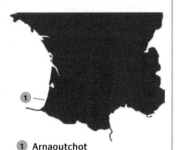

① Arnaoutchot

Arnaoutchot
www.arna.com
contact@arna.com
Tel: 00 33 558 49 11 11
Fax: 00 33 558 48 57 12
Book through France 4 Naturisme
(Suzanne Piper)

any number of **deserted beach spots** for sunning in the buff. Tourist information is available from www.leporge.fr

La Jenny naturist resort covers 300 acres and offers high quality self-catering accommodation in a choice of bungalows and houses in the woods. There are no tents or caravans. The estate has a **spectacular outdoor swimming pool** complex together with a good range of sports and entertainments. There is even a golf course. Popular with British visitors, well run and managed and a welcoming place for both first-time and experienced nudist holidaymakers alike.

St Girons Plage – Arnaoutchot

Between Bordeaux and Biarritz
Yet another outstanding bare beach on the **Aquitaine** coast, 80 kms north of the Spanish border. Arnaoutchot naturist holiday resort is located here and provides **lifeguards** on the shore to watch over the bare beachbums skinny-dipping in the Atlantic. Seamless sunbathing is on offer as far as the eye can see up and down the beach. Tourist information is available from www.tourisme-vielle-st-girons.com, www.tourismelandes.com and www.touradour.com

Travel north from **Biarritz** on the N10 to **Castets**. Turn left on to the D42 to **St Girons**. Left on to the D652 to **Vielle St Girons**, then right on to the D328 for Arnaoutchot. There is a public beach car park to the south of the resort.

Arnaoutchot naturist resort is a self-contained village with lots of accommodation to rent as well as space for tents and caravans. There are three pools, including one indoors. A health and beauty centre offers a choice of treatments. It's highly rated by regular visitors from around the world.

French naturist resorts are as good as being bare gets. **Arnaoutchot** (right) is a well-loved resort right on St Girons Plage. Picture courtesy of the resort, picture opposite Nicole Lejeune, Maison de la France (uk.franceguide.com)

1 Leucate Plage
2 St Pierre sur Mer

Oasis
www.oasis-village.com
contact@oasis-village.com
Tel: 00 33 468 40 15 17
Fax: 00 33 468 40 15 90
Peng Travel

Aphrodite
www.aphrodite-village.org
Dutch agent for bookings:
www.naturocamp.com

Ulysse
Tel: 00 33 468 40 18 39 or out of
season 00 33 468 40 99 21
Fax: 00 33 468 40 63 95
Book direct

Cailloux d'Or
www.le-guide.com/caillouxdor
caillouxdor@languedocfrance.com

La Grande Cosse
www.grandecosse.com
contact@grandecosse.com
Tel: 00 33 468 33 61 87
Fax: 00 33 468 33 32 23
Air- or rail-inclusive holidays from the
UK: Club Holidays
www.clubholiday.net

Mediterranean Beaches

Leucate Plage – Aphrodite

Port Leucate, north of Perpignan
This is a superb bare beach of fine golden sand stretching for over 1 km. The water is normally calm and the shore shelves gently into the sea making it **ideal for young families**. Occasional breezes off the Pyrenees are welcome in the summer heat.

Three established naturist resorts share the coastline here and now more nude holiday developments are springing up. However, there's still plenty of **space for everybody** on this extensive beach. Tourist info is available at www.leucate.net and www.port-leucate.com

Go north from **Perpignan** on the main N9 and turn right on to the D83, signposted Port Bacares. After 9 kms turn left on to the D627, through **Bacares**, **Port Leucate** and the bare beach is on the right. Park on the road – easy public access between Aphrodite Village and Club Oasis.

Aphrodite and **Oasis** holiday centres provide modern naturist accommodation right on the beach. Club Oasis is the newer of the two and shares facilities with the bigger Aphrodite village. In addition to all the **sports** available, there is a harbour for naked sailors to **moor boats and small yachts**. At the other end of the beach the older **Ulysse Nature** has basic apartments and camping space. There is a historic artist's house, **Cailloux d'Or**, to rent in the centre of Fitou, a small village 10 mins drive from the bare beach. The property sleeps five and has a completely private terrace and garden for all-over tanning.

St Pierre sur Mer – La Grande Cosse

Near Narbonne Plage
A lovely long undeveloped and official bare beach that has a wild feel. The sand is soft and clean, although **driftwood** is often washed up on the shore and left to bake in the sun. The **dunes, lakes and marshes** behind the beach are a haven for birds and other wildlife.

Leave **Narbonne** on the D168, travelling east to Narbonne Plage. Continue through the resort for 3 kms to **St Pierre**. There is a coastal track heading north out of the village which goes to the bare beach.

La Grande Cosse naturist camping and caravan site is located 500 metres inland from the beach. The site is popular and well equipped, offering chalets and mobile homes for hire. There is an attractive swimming pool, bar, restaurant and small grocery shop.

Serignan Plage

Near Beziers
A beautiful big bare beach lapped by the Mediterranean and popular with families. There is a **snack bar** and **lifeguard** in season. Next to the beach is the Serignan naturist holiday centre.

Exit the A9 motorway at **Beziers East**, and take the D64 towards **Serignan**. Then follow the signs to **Serignan Plage** and walk south-west along the beach.

Serignan Plage Nature is a thriving nude resort right on the beach. You can hire a range of accommodation from pre-erected furnished tents to comfy chalets and mobile homes. As well as a bar, restaurant and shop, there is even a 'casino'. Lots of on-site entertainment including a mini-club.

Cap d'Agde

Between Beziers and Sete
The most famous nude beach and resort in France which attracts up to **40,000 people** at any one time in peak season. More than 1 km of level sand and calm sea make this a popular choice for countless European nudists, although it's rather different from most of the quieter and more natural resorts and beaches. All manner of water-based activities are available.

Exit the A9 motorway at the **Agde** junction and take the RN312 expressway towards the main resort. On entering Cap d'Agde follow the signs to the **Quartier Naturiste**. There is a small charge to enter the resort. Alternatively, the bare beach

1 Serignan Plage
2 Cap d'Agde

Serignan Plage Nature
www.leserignannature.com
info@serignannaturisme.com
Tel: 00 33 467 32 09 61
Fax: 00 33 467 32 68 41
Book through France 4 Naturisme
(Suzanne Piper)

It's not a nude beach, nor a nude campsite, but an entire nudist town. **Cap d'Agde** is a huge developed resort, like any other modern tourist development but without the swimming costumes

Cap d'Agde accommodation
perso.wanadoo.fr/.agence.oltra
www.hoteleve.com
www.chm-reneoltra.com
Tour operators
Peng France, Avtravel, Through Our Eyes Travel (USA agent, website: www.cap-d-agde.com)

area can be accessed by walking south along the shore from the **Marseillan Plage** direction.

This **naked city** has apartments, villas, and a 3-star hotel, as well as camping and caravan accommodation. The whole naturist quarter is clothes-optional – so if you want it's a unique opportunity to go to the bank, have your hair cut or fuel up the car all in the buff! There is also a **marina** within the resort. Tourist info from www.capdagde.com and www.agdenaturisme.com

Les Grottes Plage, Ile du Levant

Ile du Levant, Le Lavandou

A gem of a beach on this **magical island**, reached by an easy coastal footpath 10 mins walk from the quayside. A small natural **crescent of white sand** slides gently into the turquoise sea, providing excellent swimming and snorkelling. Bare beachbums will feel like castaways at this lovely secluded cove.

There are **no private cars** allowed on the island, and the easiest way to get there is by ferry from Le Lavandou. The journey takes 35 minutes – 21 euro return (2004). The ferry timetable is published at www.vedettesilesdor.fr

Cap d'Agde's nude beach, right, has attracted millions of holidaymakers over the years. Others come for the swimming pools, restaurants, nightlife and countless other activities

Seventy years ago Ile du Levant was the **birthplace of nude leisure** in France. Today, there is a tiny resident community and lots of holiday accommodation including apartments, villas and private hotels, as well as two rustic campsites. **Minimal clothing** is normally worn in the village of Heliopolis, but gardens, sun terraces and swimming pools can be enjoyed in the buff. Tourist info from www.naturiste.com

The privately owned **Hotel Brise Marine** has 17 rooms and is near the village square. The **Villa Marie-Jeanne** self-catering studios and apartments are located half way up the hill between the village and the sea. The luxury **Hotel Ponant** has 10 rooms and is located high above the sea with spectacular views. The owners are **artists** and their works are on display throughout. The hotel offers clothes-optional sunbathing on its extensive terrace and nude swimming in the pool.

The **Residence L'Escapade** self-catering studios are located half way up the hill between the port and the village. Reasonably well placed for walking to the bare beach – 15 mins on foot. There is a large naked swimming pool. The **Hotel des Arbousiers** has eight rooms and two terraces, and is situated a couple of minutes from the centre of Heliopolis and 20 mins walk from the beach.

1 **Les Grottes Plage, Ile du Levant**

Hotel Brise Marine
www.labrisemarine.fr
info@labrisemarine.fr
Tel: 00 33 494 05 91 15
Fax: 00 33 494 05 93 21
Chalfont Holidays

Villa Marie-Jeanne
www.naturiste.com
villamariejeanne@wanadoo.fr
Tel: 00 33 494 05 99 95
Fax: 00 33 494 05 99 95
Chalfont Holidays

Hotel Ponant
www.ponant.fr
Tel: 00 33 494 05 90 41
Chalfont Holidays

Residence L'Escapade
www.escapade-levant.com
Tel: 00 33 494 05 93 45
Fax: 00 33 494 05 93 45
Book direct

Hotel des Arbousiers
http://membres.lycos.fr/arbousiers
arbousiers83@wanadoo.fr
Tel: 00 33 494 05 90 73
Book direct

1 Le Layet Plage
2 Beauvallon Plage

Grand Hotel Moriaz
www.grandhotelmoriaz.com
grand.hotel.moriaz.@wanadoo.fr
Tel: 00 33 494 05 80 01
Fax: 00 33 494 05 70 88

Le Cap Negre Hotel
www.hotel-cap-negre.com
www.lelavandou.com/hotelcapnegre
hotel-le-cap-negre@wanadoo.fr
Tel: 00 33 494 05 80 46
Fax: 00 33 494 05 89 00

Hotel Marie Louise
www.hotel-marielouise.com
hotel-marielouise@wanadoo.fr
Tel: 00 33 494 96 06 05
Fax: 00 33 494 43 96 70
Book direct

Camping Les Prairies de la Mer
www.campingazur.com
kontiki@wanadoo.fr
Tel: 00 33 494 55 96 96
Fax: 00 33 494 55 96 95
France Holidays www.france-holiday-bargains.co.uk

The French tourist office gives a high profile to France's naturist opportunities, publishing brochures, maps and website information. Picture opposite top and on pages 34-35 Nicole Lejeune, Maison de la France (uk.franceguide.com)

Le Layet Plage

Cavalière, Le Lavandou

This is a **picturesque little bare beach** tucked in a sheltered cove at the western end of Cavalière bay, by Point Layet. The sand here is soft and yellow and the sea is normally as **calm as a millpond**.

The smell of mimosa fills the air. There is an outdoor restaurant on a wooden terrace built out over the sea. This popular nude beach has a **lovely atmosphere** and gets very busy. Tourist info from www.lelavandou.com (with a picture of the nudist beach).

Drive east from **Le Lavandou** along the twisty D559 coast road and in 5 kms, just before **Cavalière**, there is a series of coves on the right. Park near the cycle tunnel and take the signposted short flight of steps down to the beach. Local information from www.lelavandou.com

The pretty seaside resort of Cavalière (not to be confused with the bigger Cavalaire along the coast) has a choice of holiday accommodation. One local hotel, about 350 metres from the bare beach, is the **Grand Hotel Moriaz**, a 3-star establishment.

The stylish family-run **Le Cap Negre Hotel** has two stars and is close to the sea at the opposite end of the bay, about 20 mins walk or 5 mins drive from the bare beach. Rooms on the top floor have small private terraces with beguiling views of the bay, framed by subtropical plants and pine trees.

Beauvallon Plage

Between Port Grimaud and St Maxime

This strand of white sand has a great location, overlooking **glamorous St Tropez** across the bay. This popular hidden beach is superb for sunning and swimming au naturel. It is only a few steps away from the road and yet **completely out of sight**.

Follow the coastal N98 east from **Port Grimaud**, passing the Camping Les Prairies de la Mer. After a further 1 km look out for a phone box above an open cove with lots of parked cars by the side of the road. Where is everybody? Walk to the breakwater on the left of the bay – they are all on the (hidden) bare beach, on the other side!

The charming 2-star **Hotel Marie Louise** at **Guerrevieille**, between Port Grimaud and St Maxime, has 12 rooms. It is a 10-minute walk from the nude beach. **Camping Les Prairies de la Mer** is a lively site situated on a sandy beach. It attracts a lot of British holidaymakers and is 20 mins walk from the bare beach, or 2 mins in the car.

Piana Verde
www.pianaverde.com
info@pianaverde.com
Tel: 00 33 495 38 82 99
Fax: 00 33 495 38 89 82
Chalfont Holidays

Bagheera
www.bagheera.fr
bagheera@bagheera.fr
Tel: 00 33 495 38 80 30
Fax: 00 33 495 38 83 47
Chalfont Holidays

Club Corsicana
www.club-corsicana.com
info@sunclubreisen.ch
Chalfont Holidays

Les Eucalyptus Camping
www.eucalyptus-camping.com
info@eucalyptus-camping.com
Tel: 00 33 495 38 87 17
Fax: 00 33 495 38 92 23
Book direct

Riva Bella
www.rivabella-corsica.com
riva-bella@wanadoo.fr
Tel: 00 33 495 38 81 10
Fax: 00 33 495 38 91 29
Book through France 4 Naturisme
(Suzanne Piper)

La Chiappa
www.chiappa.com
chiappa@wanadoo.fr
Tel: 00 33 495 70 00 31
Fax: 00 33 04 95 70 07 70
Book direct

Corsica

Bravone Plage – Piana Verde / Bagheera

East coast 50 kms south of Bastia
A wonderful **5 kms of official bare beach** with light soft sand and clear blue sea. It's so popular that five naturist resorts have been built at different points along its length. Apart from snack bars and the holiday centres there are no other developments on this **unspoilt coast**.

It is easy to find – drive 50 kms south from **Bastia** on the N198 coast road, or 70 kms north from **Porto Vecchio** on the same road. The beach is just north of **Bravone**.

The five naturist centres are: **Piana Verde** – apartments, **Bagheera** – bungalows, **Corsica Natura** – chalets, **Club Corsicana** – cabins, and **Les Eucalyptus Camping**.

Riva Bella Plage

East coast 57 kms south of Bastia
Another lovely white-sand bare beach with sunbeds and umbrellas for hire. The evocative **fragrance of the maquis** is ever present. A bar serves drinks and light meals and there's a sailing school with **wind surfers and dinghies**. The beach is home to another established naturist resort.

Signposted from the main N198 coast road, 7 kms north of the historic village of **Aleria** and 3 kms south of **Bravone**.

Riva Bella naturist resort has bungalows and apartments right on the beach. There is a wide choice of accommodation, even ready-erected 'Bengali' tents. Health and beauty treatments are available including **outdoor massages** overlooking the sea.

Porto Vecchio South – La Chiappa

South-east coast
A series of **secluded and private bare beaches** and coves, home to the clothes-optional La Chiappa Vacation Village – a daily admission fee is payable. There are lots of facilities on the main beach, and the whole area is in a protected zone. Plenty of **coastline to explore**, in the buff if you wish.

Travel south from **Porto Vecchio** on the main N198 for 2 kms. Turn left at the signpost for **Chiappa Lighthouse** and **Plage de Palombaggia**. Continue for 8 kms along a twisty minor road to the entrance of the resort.

La Chiappa Vacation Village attracts discerning visitors from across Europe. A big swimming pool right by the main beach and a tennis school are just two of many attractions at this well-equipped holiday centre.

Porto Vecchio North – Villata

South-east coast

A beautiful sandy bare bay overlooking Pinarellu Island and lapped by a tranquil aquamarine sea. The famous nudist film, 'Travelling Light', was shot on location here in the late 1950s. Views inland include **breathtaking mountain peaks**, frequently snow-capped as late as June.

At the southern end of the bay there is a deliciously **romantic natural rock pool** for swimming or just soaking. The transparent water and rocky headlands make the sea here ideal for **snorkelling**. Villata naturist campsite is right by the beach so refreshments are available and there are sunbeds for hire.

Travel north from **Porto Vecchio**, firstly on the D568 coast road, then the D468 towards **Pinarellu**. After travelling 10 kms from Porto Vecchio watch out for signs and a right turn to **Villata** (3 kms before Pinarellu).

1 Bravone Plage
2 Riva Bella Plage
3 Porto Vecchio North
4 Porto Vecchio South

If you think spas are a good way to unwind, try a spa next to a nude beach for a completely natural experience. **Riva Bella** is a resort that combines the best of both in a peaceful naturist environment

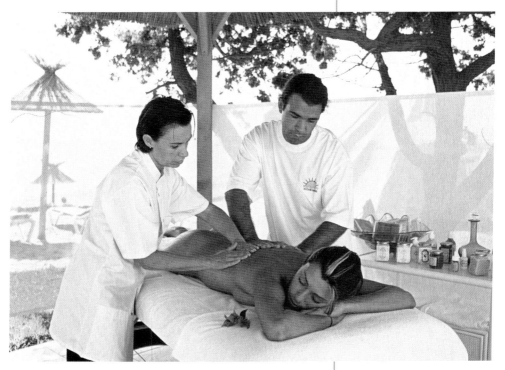

Villata Naturist Centre
www.villata.com
villata@free.fr
Tel: 00 33 495 71 62 90
Fax: 00 33 495 71 61 33
Book direct

Villata Naturist Centre has plenty of camping space and basic bungalows to rent. The estate is set in extensive pinewoods that cascade right down to the sea.

The setting is particularly attractive, with a complete 'away from it all' feeling, even though the exclusive seaside town of Porto Vecchio is not far away. A 15-minute drive inland will take you into the foothills, where skinny-dipping in **clear mountain rivers** can be enjoyed.

An idyllic spot, right, near the source of the Furcone river at **U Furu naturist centre**, 8 kms inland from Porto Vecchio. There are many other inviting streams and rivers nearby just waiting to be explored au naturel. Info from www.u-furu.com

Bare living

The beautiful beaches in this book make being bare outdoors a truly fabulous experience. Some visitors love it so much they want to revel in the freedom all holiday.

The French have perfected the art of being bare on holiday with some of Europe's most peaceful and stress-free resorts built around their coast and countryside. Spain, Greece and Croatia also have their very own naturist holiday villages.

So if you want a holiday where you can live naked, the choices stretch from peaceful campsites to luxury hotels, spa and health resorts. If you're curious rather than convinced, almost all are built around a public bare beach where you can simply go for a swim and a sunbathe without staying.

And you don't have to become a devoted naturist if you want to stay for more. Millions of people go just because you simply wear what makes you most comfortable. People get dressed in the evenings, like at any other beach resort.

In fact if you like camping holidays, going naked is a natural extension of living the outdoor life. Some guidebooks even recommend naturist campsites simply because they are just that bit nicer than ordinary ones. These are places where bare is just a better alternative to a bikini. There's literally nothing more to it than that.

Spain

Spain mainland

The popularity of bare beaches has taken off in Spain in just a single generation. Although something of a late starter compared to other European countries, it has been making up for lost time since it gained its first official nude beach in 1979. The Spanish are now amongst the most enthusiastic and progressive advocates of the bare beach lifestyle.

It is good news for holidaymakers – and of course for the tourist industry that knows a good thing when it sees it. Spain has expanded its bare bathing facilities on a breathtaking scale, and continues to develop apace.

There is a huge choice of places to stay near many of the bare beaches, including some hotels with nude terraces. Several are listed in this guide. There are also some lovely naturist resorts, particularly in the hot and sunny south of the country, where the sun shines brightly for much of the year and the clothes are off whenever you want.

Spain is easy and cheap to reach from Britain and many of us are now taking full advantage of the growing number of charter and low-cost airlines that fly there every day. If you'd never imagined you could take a beach mini-break without packing a bikini... look at Spain and think again.

Costa de la Luz

Playa de Castilla South

Matalascanas, Huelva

The **longest and most solitary** sandy beach in southern Spain. The 20 kms of shoreline is part of the Donana National Park, famous for flamingos. There are no proper roads behind the coast so by walking a short distance you can have as much beach to yourself as you want in this bare haven.

Drive south-east from Huelva for 40 kms on the C442 coast road to the resorts of **Torre de la Higuera** and then **Matalascanas**. Walk south down the beach.

1 Playa de Castilla South
2 Cabo de Trafalgar North
3 Canos de Meca

Cabo de Trafalgar North

Canos de Meca, Barbate

A fantastic **huge sweeping beach** of almost white sand, stretching for miles. The Atlantic ocean rolls up on this beautifully unspoilt coastline and there is space enough for everyone. The dress code is completely relaxed and beachgoers will be a mix of those in the buff and those wearing swimsuits.

It's easy to find. On the coast road 1 km north of **Canos de Meca** turn left at the sign to **Cabo de Trafalgar**. After 700 metres, park below the lighthouse and walk to the beach on the right (north).

The **Hostal La Aceitera** is a small family-run rural property approached along a short unmade track off the coast road. The clothes-optional beach is 300 metres walk.

The **Hostal Mini Golf** is a modern 1-star pension with a choice of accommodation including ensuite rooms, self-catering apartments and detached chalets. Located by the turn to the lighthouse at Cabo de Trafalgar. According to the hostal website: 'These beaches are considered the most virgin in the area, where nudism surprises no one.'

Hostal La Aceitera
www.miraalsur.com/aceitera/hotel
Tel: 00 34 956 43 70 16
Mobile: 00 34 676 61 55 68
Book direct

Hostal Mini Golf
www.hostalminigolf.com
info@hostalminigolf.com
Tel: 00 34 956 43 70 83
Fax: 00 34 956 43 73 65
Book direct

Whatever you want: Spain and the Spanish islands have more choice than any other bare beach destination

Canos de Meca

Canos de Meca, Barbate

This is a picturesque and popular **golden sandy beach**

Hostel Mar de Frente
www.miraalsur.com/mardefrente
Tel/Fax: 00 34 956 43 72 91
Mobile: 00 34 661 86 13 31
Book direct

Costa Natura
www.costanatura.com
info@costanatura.com
Tel: 00 34 952 80 80 65
Fax: 00 34 952 80 80 74
Peng Travel

Costa Natura – Apartment B91
malcolm@phillipgoodwin.fsnet.co.uk
Tel: 01895 232231 (UK)
Fax: 01895 233015 (UK)
Book direct

Hotel Elba and Spa
www.hoteleselba.com
elbaestepona@hoteleselba.com
Tel: 00 34 952 79 43 08
Fax: 00 34 952 79 39 57
Cadogan

Hotel Paraiso
www.golftravel4u.com/hotelproofs/
27paraiso.html
hparaiso@spa.es
Tel: 00 34 952 88 30 00
Fax: 00 34 952 88 20 19
Thomson, JMC Select, Mundi Color

Almanat beach, below, is by a handy naturist resort. There is a car park if you only want to visit the beach

backed by natural low cliffs on the edge of the Brena Natural Park. A friendly atmosphere is always apparent on this traditionally bare beach, which is particularly popular with **young people**.

Drive south through the village of **Canos de Meca** to the end of the road by the Hostal Mar Frente. A path and steps lead down to the beach in less than two minutes.

The newly built (2002) **Hostel Mar de Frente** is extremely stylish, well beyond its 2-star rating, and has its own private steps to the clothes-optional beach.

Costa del Sol

Costa Natura

Estepona

As Spain's **first 'official' nude beach**, authorised in 1979, Costa Natura is now a firmly established and well-known bare beach. It is normally busy in high season and the lively bar serves a good selection of drinks and snacks. Sunbeds and umbrellas are also available to rent. The beach is directly in front of the naturist resort of the same name.

Head south-west out of **Estepona** for 3 kms towards Gibraltar on the N340 coast road and Costa Natura is on the left. Public access to the beach is possible either side of the resort.

Costa Natura has 200 privately owned apartments set in delightful subtropical naturist gardens next to the nude beach. The properties are designed in the style of a typical white Andalusian village and enjoy super coastal and mountain views.

Costa Natura – **Apartment B91** is a recommended British owned property with a big private panoramic first-floor terrace, perfect for outdoor living. The spacious accommodation is airy and light.

The new 5-star **Hotel Elba and Spa** next door to Costa Natura opens in June 2004. It is located on the beach, and is less than 100 metres from the nudist section. For that pampered experience the spa will offer a choice of health and beauty treatments.

The 4-star **Hotel Paraiso** at Estepona is a golfing hotel set inland but with views of the sea. There is a nudist solarium for sunbathing on the fourth floor. The hotel is situated towards Marbella, a short drive from Costa Natura.

www.barebeaches.com

Cabopino Playa

Puerto Cabopino, Calahonda

A super biscuit-coloured sand beach, unusual on this part of the Costa del Sol. Backed by **extensive dunes and pine trees**, the shore is clothes-optional for up to 700 metres. One area is good for skinny-dipping, but beware – other parts have submerged rocks. There is a **beach bar**, where it's normal to wear light clothing. Don't let reports of 'cruising' men and couples in the dunes put you off enjoying this place. They shouldn't interfere with your relaxation on the actual beach itself.

Mid-way between **Marbella** and **Fuengirola** on the N340 coast road – look out for signs to Puerto Cabopino. In half a kilometre, just before entering the port, turn right into the car park and drive along the sandy track to Las Dunas bar at the clothes-optional beach. Alternatively, stop earlier and walk through the pines and over the dunes – there are lots of paths.

Cabopino Camping is a well-equipped, good quality site just 1 km from the bare beach. Bungalows and cabins are available to rent as well as pitches for tents and caravans. There are two outdoor pools and plans for a new indoor one in 2004. Plenty of sports facilities available.

1 Costa Natura
2 Cabopino Playa

Cabopino Camping
www.campingcabopino.com
info@cabopino.com
Book direct

Cabopino beach, below, is a popular spot year round thanks to the Costa del Sol's fabulous climate

1. Benalnatura Beach
2. Almanat Beach
3. Cantarrijan Playa

Benalnatura beach in the centre of the Costa del Sol is a great place to get an all-over tan

Benalnatura beach

Benalmadena

A cosy little cove right in the heart of the Costa del Sol, with a sheltered aspect making it ideal for **winter sunning**. The beach is well cared for by the bar owner, who has provided toilets and showers. It's only 150 metres long so during summer get there early if you want a good spot.

On the western side of **Benalmadena**, 2 kms from the marina, towards **Fuengirola** on the N340 coast road. The path with easy steps to the beach is signposted off the access road.

The 3-star **Flatotel International** apartments offer some of the nearest holiday accommodation and also provide a good landmark. Travelling from Benalmadena the apartments are 250 metres before the beach. There is a bus stop outside the Flatotel.

The 4-star **Hotel Playabonita** is 600 metres from Benalnatura, along the coast road in the direction of Fuengirola. Right next door is the 3-star **Costa Marina Apartotel** which overlooks the sea. It is 700 metres from the bare beach. The 5-star **Hotel Torrequebrada** is 750 metres from Benalnatura nude beach.

A self-contained luxury **apartment in Mijas**, which is part of the home of a Scottish naturist couple, has a skinny-dipping swimming pool and spa pool in the garden, and is 15 mins drive from Benalnatura

Finca Los Etera at Alora, near Malaga, is a 300-year-old traditional farmhouse a 30-minute drive from the nude beaches. There are five en-suite rooms and board is all-inclusive. Owners Nigel and Nikki are naturists and the pool and grounds are clothes-optional.

Almanat Beach

Just outside Torre del Mar
It might not be the prettiest spot in the world with light grey shingle and sand, but it is one of the most **popular and practical** bare beaches in the area. There's a car park right next to it (small charge). Long beach walks are on offer in the bare section as well as a **nudist bar** serving a good choice of food. Sunbeds and umbrellas are available to rent.

Travelling towards **Malaga** on the N340, 2 kms west of Torre del Mar, the turn to the beach and campsite is clearly signposted. A short lane through market garden crops brings you to the camp site and parking in 600 metres.

Camping Almanat naturist site by the beach is well equipped and has a big attractive swimming pool. New residential chalets for hire. In winter the site is popular with long-stay visitors (snowbirds) from northern Europe.

Costa Tropical

Cantarrijan Playa

Between Nerja and Almunecar
Not one but two delightful buff beaches, popular with **locals and holidaymakers** alike. You can drive right up to the first one, where there is a pair of fine restaurants as well as sunbeds, umbrellas and pedalos for hire. The second (secret) beach is a few steps away, round the corner to the left as you face the sea. Here you will find a **totally undeveloped and much bigger** stretch of sand and shingle.

It feels a million miles away from civilisation – all the beach users are completely bare and there's nothing else besides. Sheltered from the wind, it gets really warm and is **used all year**. The whole bay is unspoilt and backed by picturesque tree-covered hills rising steeply from the coast.

Travel east from **Nerja** on the N340, and in 10 kms the road

Flatotel International
www.flatotelcostadelsol.com
info@flatotelcostadelsol.com
Tel: 00 34 952 44 58 00
Fax: 00 34 952 44 04 67
Libra Holidays, Stein Travel (Ireland), Holiday Hotels

Hotel Playabonita
www.hotelesplaya.com
playabonita@hotelesplaya.com
Tel: 00 34 952 44 28 40
Fax: 00 34 950 33 36 55 (central reservations)
Airtours, Mundi Color, Hvsl.es

Costa Marina Apartotel
www.costamarinaapartotel.com
luchy@costamarinaapartotel.com
Tel: 00 34 952 57 71 21
Fax: 00 34 952 56 24 61
Libra, Holidayhotels.co.uk

Hotel Torrequebrada
www.torrequebrada.com
comercial@torrequebrada.com
Tel: 00 34 952 44 60 00
Fax: 00 34 952 44 57 02
Thomson, Mundi Color, Holiday Hotels, Medhotels.com

Mijas apartment
sheonadoug@hotmail.com
Tel: 01890 751821 (UK)
Fax: 01890 750176 (UK)
Tel: 00 34 952 59 10 88 or
00 34 655 75 48 25-6
Book direct

Finca Los Etera
www.fincalosetera.net
fincalosetera@msn.com
Tel: 00 34 952 11 26 20
Book direct

Camping Almanat
www.almanat.de
info@almanat.de
Tel: 00 34 952 55 62 71
Fax: 00 34 952 55 62 71
Book direct

Eagle Peak
www.eaglepeakspain.com
info@eaglepeakspain.com
Tel: 00 34 958 63 94 92
Fax: 00 34 958 63 94 76
Book direct with Peter and Liz

crosses a viaduct marking the boundary between the provinces of Malaga and Granada. In 1 km turn into the lay-by on the right with the big sign 'Almunecar La Herradura'. From there follow the small sign down to the beach, which is reached after 1.5 kms of unmade road.

There is little accommodation locally because of the area's protected natural status. However, a good choice would be **Eagle Peak** clothes-optional apartments, 20 mins drive away – see Playa del Muerto.

Playa del Muerto

Almunecar
A pleasant undeveloped beach of sand and shingle, officially nudist and easy to reach. At more than 500 metres long there will be **room for everyone** and the beach rarely gets too crowded. Remember to take your refreshments with you, or alternatively pop back into town for a drink.

Head west along the seafront out of **Almunecar** and in 2 kms, at **Cotobro**, the road turns inland. Park here and the path to the bare beach is signposted round the next headland via a promenade, no more than 5 mins walk from the car.

Cantarrijan beach is a lovely bare beach, with handy nude-friendly accommodation nearby at Eagle Peak

Eagle Peak clothing-optional apartments, located on high ground at Cotobro, Almunecar, overlook the coastline and Playa del Muerto. There are six good quality properties and a panoramic terrace on the roof. Owners Peter and Liz offer Landrover **trips into the mountains** for bare walks and skinny-dipping in the natural pools, at no extra charge. Also, buff trips round the bay in Peter's inflatable powerboat. The largest lemons you'll ever see grow in the **tropical garden** – help yourself. Playa del Muerto is 15 mins walk or 5 mins in the car. Cantarrijan nude beach is 20 mins drive.

① Playa del Muerto
② Playa Cerrillos
③ Playa Cabo de Gata

Costa Almeria

Playa Cerrillos

Roquetas de Mar
A long sand and shingle beach that feels remote, where it's easy to find space for yourself. You might encounter the **occasional fisherman**, but he is unlikely to disturb you. The immediate area is low-lying and cooling breezes will be welcome in the height of summer.

The bare beach is an extension of **Roquetas de Mar** town beach, heading south-west past **Playa Serena**. You can walk along the shore or take the lane running between the sea and the salt flats.

Hotel Playacapricho is a large 4-star property in Roquetas, which has a nude sun terrace. The 3-star **Hotel Playatropical** at Aguadulce is on the beach in the tranquil bay of El Palmer, 8 kms north of Roquetas. There's a small naturist beach within a short walk at Enix Playa.

Hotel Playacapricho
www.hotelesplaya.com
capricho@hotelesplaya.com
Tel: 00 34 950 33 31 00
Fax: 00 34 950 33 36 55
(central reservations)
Airtours, Mundi Color

Hotel Playatropical
www.hotelesplaya.com
tropical@hotelesplaya.com
Tel: 00 34 950 34 05 00
Fax: 00 34 950 33 36 55
(central reservations) Mundi Color

Playa del Muerto, handy for Eagle Peak apartments above the beach

Playa Cabo de Gata

Cabo de Gata village (not the lighthouse of the same name)
Miles of level dark sand and shingle make up this impressive undeveloped bare beach, which has **easy access** from the road. Swimming is good and the sea can be calmer than other nearby coasts. Beach users will usually be a **harmonious mix** of

swimsuited and nudist, and with plenty of room you will easily find your own spot.

From **Almeria City** head east, past the airport along the coast to the fishing village of **Cabo de Gata**. Go through the village and park anywhere along the road to **La Almadraba de Monteleva**. The beach is accessed by one of the many short boardwalks.

Playa de Monsul

South of San Jose

This is a lovely unspoilt area within the Cabo de Gata Natural Park. A **huge sand dune** on the north side of Playa de Monsul makes an impressive landmark. Bare beachbums usually head for the opposite side of the bay, which is more secluded. The next beach to the south, **Ensenada de la Media Luna**, is also very popular for naked bathing. The **soft golden sand** makes swimming a delight, provided the sea is calm. This is **protected virgin country** – no beach bars, so bring your own refreshments because it can be extremely hot in mid-summer.

From the small fishing port and resort of **San Jose** take the unsurfaced road south towards the **Cabo de Gata** lighthouse,

Vera Playa beach, below and right, has seen huge expansion in recent years with accommodation being built to keep up with the rapid growth in bare beach visitors

past the attractive **Playa de los Genoveses** (some buff bathing towards southern end). The main track continues to Playa de Monsul. It is 3.5 kms from **St Jose** and there is plenty of parking.

Vera Playa

Between Garrucha and Villaricos

This is Spain's **capital of nudism**. A long wide beach with a big choice of naturist accommodation next to it. Great for au naturel sunning, walking and skinny-dipping. Beach bars, sunbeds, pedalos, volleyball – **it's got it all**. Busy in summer but still easy to find a quieter place to yourself. Almeria has the **hottest and driest** climate in the country, so the beach season is long – in fact anything up to 12 months. Most European nationalities come and chill out here, giving it a really **cosmopolitan** and friendly atmosphere.

Take the coast road north from **Garrucha**, through **Puerto Rey** and Vera Playa is well signposted in a further 1.5 kms.

A whole bare community has developed over the years offering every type of holiday from camping and caravanning, through self-catering, to a **luxury nude hotel**. Ongoing

1 Playa de Monsul
2 Vera Playa

Hotel Vera Playa
www.hotelesplaya.com
vera@hotelesplaya.com
Tel: 00 34 950 46 74 75
Fax: 00 34 950 33 36 55
(central reservations)
Mundi Color, Peng Travel

Vera Natura and La Menara
www.veranatura.com
veranatura@veranatura.com
Tel: 00 34 950 46 73 84
Canarian Dreams, Peng Travel

Bahia de Vera
www.bahiadevera.com
mail@bahiadevera.com
Canarian Dreams

Torremar Natura
www.keymare.com
www.its-natural.net

Natsun apartments
natsun.com/refres.htm
jvstuyvesant@natsun.com
Tel: 00 34 950 46 70 27
Fax: 00 34 950 46 70 28

Parque Vera
www.verplaya.info
www.parquevera.com

Camping Almanzora
www.campings.net/almanzora
almanzora@campings.net
Tel: 00 34 950 46 74 25

Game on: **El Portus**, right, has a bare beach backed up by a great resort where you can drop your clothes and your cares at the door. Pictures supplied by the resort

construction. Two general information websites are www.veraplaya.info and www.naturistspain.com

Hotel Vera Playa is right on the beach and probably unique not only in Spain but in the world. Although offering similar high standards of service to thousands of other big 4-star holiday hotels, it's the only one that is naturist. But it's OK to dress up smartly in the evening, because clothes are required after 8 pm. The hotel is closed in the winter.

Vera Natura and **La Menara** apartments provide well-equipped naturist holiday accommodation with skinny-dipping pools in the gardens. Vera Natura is on the bare beach and the newer La Menara development is set further back. **Bahia de Vera** apartments are spacious and have large outdoor terraces. There are indoor and outdoor pools, as well as tennis, volleyball and a gymnasium. The bare beach is 150 metres away.

Torremar Natura apartments are some of the newest, set back a short distance from the beach. The last phase is due to be completed in 2004. There is a swimming pool. **Natsun** apartments range from original 1980s (El Cano 1) to brand new (El Cano 3), basic to luxury, with some right on the beach. **Vera Luz** apartments are also part of Natsun. Dutch developer Jan Stuyvesant and his family have been building and renting naturist accommodation here for more than 20 years.

Parque Vera consists of townhouses and large blocks of apartments set in gardens with swimming pools. The bare beach is close by. Most have private Spanish owners.

Camping Almanzora naturist site for tents and caravans is popular all year round. It has a swimming pool and is close to the shops and restaurants. It is only a few steps away from the bare beach.

Costa Calida

Bolnuevo Beaches

Near Puerto de Mazarron
A string of undeveloped sand and shingle official nude beaches, which become less inhabited the further you travel from town. Set in **wild countryside** there is little to disturb the bare beach enthusiast on these remote shores.

From **Puerto de Mazarron** head south along the coast through the suburbs towards the village of **Bolnuevo**. Signs for Playa Nudista can be spotted along the way. Continue through Bolnuevo to a small roundabout, where an unsurfaced road continues along the coast. After the first cove all are bare beaches.

El Portus

Portus, near Cartagena
An idyllic official nude bay surrounded by **mountains** that appear to rise straight out of the sea. The beach is a mix of dark sand and pebbles and the **swimming is first class** – ideal for snorkelling. Often more sheltered than other places and popular throughout the year.

Travel south from **Cartagena** on the local road through

1 Bolnuevo Beaches
2 El Portus

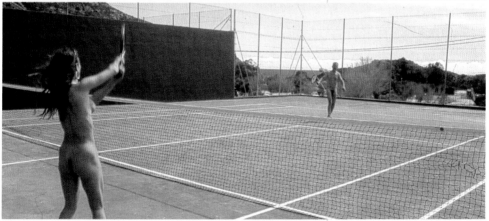

1 Playa Negrete

2 Playa los Tusales

Camping Naturista El Portus
www.elportus.com
elportus@elportus.com
Tel: 00 34 968 55 30 52
Fax: 00 34 968 55 30 53
Away With Dune

Hotel Hyatt and Las Lomas Apartments
www.lamanga.hyatt.com
lamanga@hyattintl.com
Tel: 00 34 968 33 12 34
Fax: 00 34 968 33 12 35
Sovereign, Real Spain, Thomas Cook

El Portus beach, right, is popular with bare beach lovers from across Europe. Picture supplied by Camping Naturista El Portus

Canteras. After 7 kms from the city take the left turn to El Portus, which is a further 4 kms. The large bare bay is next to the smaller village beach and is easy to access through the campsite.

Camping Naturista El Portus is next to the beach, with rugged grounds extending to a million square metres up the hillside. There are super indoor and outdoor pools, a restaurant, a shop and plenty of caravan and chalet accommodation. The resort is popular with naturist families from all over Europe and the whole area is totally unspoilt. As a testimony to the fine winter weather the site is open all year. Alicante and Murcia are the nearest airports.

Playa Negrete

Calblanque, La Manga

A series of lovely long **gold and ochre coloured** sandy beaches in the picturesque Calblanque Regional Park. Playa Negrete is the most popular with bare beachbums, but the others, including Playa Calblanque, are generally considered clothes-optional as well. Easily **accessible by car or bicycle**.

Travel east on the main dual carriageway MU312 approaching **La Manga**, and exit at the signs for **Playa Calblanque** and **Los Balones**. Follow the road along the side of the highway and turn right at the **Calblanque Parque** sign. It's a short drive through the park to the beaches – Playa Negrete is towards the west. The park rangers **welcome nudist visitors** so don't hesitate to ask for advice or directions.

The renowned golf and sports resort at La Manga is 10 mins drive from the beach and has a range of places to stay including apartments, private villas and a deluxe hotel.

The 5-star **Hotel Hyatt and Las Lomas Apartments** have a health and beauty spa together with indoor and outdoor swimming pools.

Costa Blanca

Playa los Tusales

La Marina, Guardamar del Segura

A long pale sandy nude beach backed by **dunes and pinewoods**. Popular with families, this delightfully unspoilt beach has more than 2 kms for bare bathing – room for everybody to find their own space.

Drive south from **Alicante**, through **Santa Pola** on the N332 to La Marina. Turn left down the lane next to **Camping Internacional** and in 1.5 kms at the car park turn right. From

**Camping Internacional
La Marina**
www.camping-lamarina.com
info@camping-lamarina.com
Book direct

the end of the car park, south to the mouth of the river Segura, the beach is au naturel.

Camping Internacional La Marina is ideal and only 10 mins walk from the bare beach. It has the maximum 5-star quality grading and offers a wide range of facilities including bungalows for hire. There is a good local bus service from the entrance.

Playa El Carabassi

Gran Alacant

This **broad sandy beach** backed by extensive dunes is near a large number of new holiday homes currently being built in the area. Towards the southern end of the beach official signs advise 'Playa Nudista'.

Travel south from **Alicante** on the N332 past the airport then after a further 3.5 kms by the Repsol garage take the slip road on right and flyover for **Gran Alacant**. Drive straight through the small town and down a steep hill to the beach. At the T junction cross over the road into the car park, keep right and the bare area is to your right as you face the sea – simply look for the sign.

Montiboli Hotel
www.servigroup.es
montiboli@servigroup.es
Tel: 00 34 965 89 02 50
Fax: 00 34 965 89 38 57
JMC Select, Thomson a la Carte,
Mundi Color, Real Spain

**Euro Tennis Hotel
and Apartments**
www.hoteleurotennis.com
reserves@hoteleurotennis.com
Tel: 00 34 965 89 12 50
Fax: 00 34 965 89 11 94
Mundi Color

Playa del Esparello

Montiboli, Villajoyosa

An attractive, large but **fairly secluded pebble cove** situated outside town. Although not far from **Benidorm** this spot feels a world away. It is an official nude beach with good swimming. The edge of the next cove, **La Caleta**, is occasionally used for bare bathing.

Travel south from the resort of **Villajoyosa** along the N332 and in 3 kms turn left signposted Hotel Montiboli. Then bear left into a cul de sac going down to the beach about 0.5 km before the hotel.

The exclusive 5-star **Montiboli Hotel** is set on a low promontory between the two coves. Rooms 21-27 on the top floor directly **overlook the nude beach** and have large private terraces ideal for sunbathing in the buff.

The 3-star **Euro Tennis Hotel and Apartments**, accommodating 400 people, is next to Hotel Montiboli and located directly behind Playa La Caleta. It is 10-15 mins walk or 3 mins drive to Playa del Esparello.

Cumbre del Sol

Moraira, near Javea (Xabia)

A popular 450-metre shingle beach surrounded by huge cliffs. It is usually **sheltered and warm**, providing good swimming from the steeply shelving shore. There is a bar serving refreshments at one end of the bay and the bare beach users mostly go to the other end.

From **Javea** use the local roads south to **Benitachell** village, then follow signs to **Cumbre del Sol** and finally down the steep hill to the car park by the beach.

The **Casa Natura B&B** guesthouse provides nudist accommodation and has four rooms to let. It is set in pretty subtropical gardens, complete with pool, terraces and a boules court. 15-20 mins drive from Cumbre del Sol bare beach.

Costa Dorada

Playa El Torn

L'Hospitalet de L'Infant (Tarragona)
A beautiful and popular yellow sandy bare beach 1.5 kms long, enclosed by **rocky headlands** at each end. There is a bar selling refreshments and snacks but little other development by this

1 Playa El Carabassi
2 Playa del Esparello
3 Cumbre del Sol
4 Playa El Torn

Casa Natura B&B
www.chalfontholidays.co.uk
info@chalfontholidays.co.uk
Tel: 00 34 966 46 02 99
Chalfont Holidays or book directly
with owners Rod and Pauline

① Playa de Pals

El Templo del Sol
www.eltemplodelsol.com
info@eltemplodelsol.net
Tel: 00 34 977 82 34 34
Fax: 00 34 977 81 13 06
Book direct

Camping Relax Nat
www.campingrelaxnat.com
info@relaxnat.com
Tel: 00 34 972 30 08 18
Fax: 00 34 972 60 11 00
Book direct

Pals beach, below and overleaf, on the Costa Brava is a great draw for bare beach fans. Picture overleaf from the Spanish Tourist Office (Turespaña) www.tourspain.es

lovely **pine-scented coastline**. There's a lifeguard and first aid post and it's **great for families**.

Travelling on N340 locate the km marker post 1130 and turn for **L'Hospitalet**. A small road runs south by the beach to the car park just after the railway crossing – there is a parking fee. Only 20 mins from **Reus Airport**.

The **El Templo del Sol** naturist camping and caravan site is modern and well equipped. There is a particularly impressive swimming pool as well as lots of other sports and entertainment facilities. It has direct access to the nude beach.

Costa Brava

Playa de Pals

Pals, near Palafrugell

Two **super, official nudist coves** at the southern end of the 4 km Playa de Pals. Although some bare sunseekers use the main beach, most buff bathers head for one of the two small bays. Popular with locals and holidaymakers, there's always a lively atmosphere.

Travel north from **Palafrugell** towards **Pals** and watch for the sign to **Platja de Pals**. The red and white painted radio mast near the beach is a good landmark. Park at the southern end and walk round to the coves.

Camping Relax Nat is a lovely family orientated site for nudists with three swimming pools and bungalows to rent. Located between Palafrugell and Palamos, less than 5 kms from the sea and a short drive to the bare beach.

Canary Islands

Fuerteventura's beaches are
beautifully bare, in every sense.
You might be the only naked
soul on **El Cotillo surf beach**,
on the island's north-west coast

Canary Islands

The Canary islands are a favourite winter playground for the British. It's just four hours' flight from the grind of dark damp days and long cold nights to the bliss of warm sub-tropical sunshine. Best of all there are countless beaches where you can strip off and go as nature intended. Choose whichever colour of sand you like – there's every shade from volcanic black to sun-bleached white!

Fuerteventura is especially well known for its beautiful pristine shores and a completely laid-back attitude to nudity. Not to be out done, Lanzarote, Gran Canaria and La Gomera provide a host of options for finding your own bare space by the sea. Tenerife has a choice of reasonably priced 4- and 5-star hotels with au naturel sun terraces and pools for skinny-dipping, if you prefer a little deluxe de-clothing.

Fuerteventura

Corralejo dunes beach

Four kilometres south of Corralejo

The dunes provide a spectacular backdrop to a **line of yellow sandy beaches** with great views across the bay. Although popular, there is plenty of space for that away-from-it-all feeling. You will find a relaxed mix of swimsuited and bare bathers.

The **main road south** from Corralejo to Puerto del Rosario runs right by the beach and dunes 4 kms outside town, and there is plenty of parking by the side of the road. Buses and taxis are readily available.

Two large comfortable **hotels** and an **apartment complex** have been built close together on the dunes. **Hotel Riu Palace Tres Islas** is a 4-star hotel and next to it is the 3-star **Hotel Riu Oliva Beach**. The **Oliva Beach Apartments** are set back slightly from the sea. The beach is clothes-optional within 200m north or south of the hotels and apartments. The **Infiniti Apartments** are new, high-quality apartments and villas on the outskirts of Corralejo with rooftop sauna and a solarium for bare sunbathing. A further 10 kms south of Corralejo, the luxury **Villa Bougainvillaea** has two bedrooms and a secluded pool and large terrace perfect for bare bathing.

Corallejo dunes beach, below and on left, has a good view of the intriguing volcanic island of Lobos – and plenty of space to lose yourself in the golden dunes. Fuerteventura is famed for its strong winds but there are shelters along the beaches. It is a hugely popular destination for nude beach lovers and the hotels are keen to attract their share of the island's visitors. Many are either right by the nude beaches or have their own nude bathing facilities.

① Corralejo dunes beach

Hotel Riu Palace Tres Islas
www.riu.com
palace.tresilas@riu.com
Tel: 00 34 928 53 57 00
Fax: 00 34 928 53 58 58
JMC, Thomson a la Carte, Mundi Color, Sovereign, Cosmos

Hotel Riu Oliva Beach
www.riu.com
hotel.olivabeach@riu.com
Tel: 00 34 928 53 53 34
Fax: 00 34 928 86 61 54
Unijet, JMC, Mundi Color, Thomas Cook, Medhotels.com

Oliva Beach Apartments
www.riu.com
apartamentos.olivabeach@riu.com
Tel: 00 34 928 53 56 96
Fax: 00 34 928 53 56 69
Airtours, Thomas Cook, JMC

Infiniti Apartments
www.infiniticorralejo.co.uk
enquiries@infiniticorralejo.co.uk
Tel: 01548 561289 (UK)
Island Seekers or book direct

Villa Bougainvillaea
www.islandseekers.co.uk
enquiry@islandseekers.co.uk
Tel: 01787 281417 (UK)
Fax: 01787 281526 (UK)
Island Seekers, Sunseekers

El Caleton apartments
www.islandseekers.co.uk
enquiry@islandseekers.co.uk
Tel: 01787 281417 (UK)
Fax: 01787 281526 (UK)

Maravilla apartments
www.islandseekers.co.uk
enquiry@islandseekers.co.uk
Tel: 01787 281417 (UK)
Fax: 01787 281526 (UK)
Island Seekers, Sunseekers

El Balcon del Cotillo apartments
www.sunseekerholidays.com
sunseekers@dial.pipex.com
Tel: 08700 660 480 (UK)
Fax: 01403 891 059 (UK)

Villa Demelza
www.islandseekers.co.uk
enquiry@islandseekers.co.uk
Tel: 01787 281417 (UK)
Fax: 01787 281526 (UK)
Travellers Way, Island Seekers

El Cotillo lagoons beaches

Five hundred metres north of El Cotillo

A cluster of **picturesque sandy coves** divided by low volcanic rocks. The turquoise seawater pools are protected by offshore reefs, making them perfect for swimming and snorkelling. The coves are popular for getting that all-over tan, or bare walks between bays.

El Cotillo is on the **north-west coast**, 20 minutes' drive from Corralejo. There is a newly surfaced road heading north from the village towards the lighthouse. The beaches are on the left-hand side and are used bare from within half a kilometre, stretching into the distance. Parking by the beaches. There are buses from Corralejo to El Cotillo.

El Caleton apartments are on the beach in an unspoilt spot with 11 units about 1 km from the village. Nude sunbathing is available a few steps from your door. **Maravilla apartments** are a few minutes' walk from the nearest clothes-optional areas. There is a small sheltered swimming pool. **El Balcon del Cotillo apartments** provide basic one-bedroom accommodation on the beach, half a kilometre from the village and less than five minutes' walk to the bare area. The recently built three-bedroom **Villa**

Demelza is in a rural setting outside Lajares. The swimming pool and terrace are secluded for sunbathing and swimming sans costume. The bare beaches at El Cotillo are 10 kms by car or bus.

Lighthouse beaches

Two kilometres north of El Cotillo

These **wild and remote** coves towards the northern tip of Fuerteventura, next to the El Cotillo beaches, have some **stunning white sand**. Although the sea crashes dramatically on the rocky headlands, the water in the coves is normally sheltered and calm. Ideal for finding your own **peace and tranquillity**.

Take the **road north** out of El Cotillo for almost 2 kms, passing the lagoons beaches on the left. Approaching the lighthouse, there is a sandy track off to the right. The coves appear within a few hundred metres. Ordinary cars might be seen negotiating the final part of the track, but soft sand and rough terrain make it more appropriate for off-road vehicles. The best beaches are nearer the lighthouse.

El Cotillo surf beach

On the southern edge of El Cotillo

A **big and ruggedly attractive** beach, popular with windsurfers. It is rarely busy and there is plenty of space for bare sunseekers. However, care should be taken when swimming because of the undertow.

It couldn't be easier to find because it is right on the **southern outskirts** of the village, reached by a wide track. Parking is on the low cliff above the beach with an easy scramble down to the sand.

① El Cotillo lagoons beach
② Lighthouse beaches
③ El Cotillo surf beach

El Cotillo lagoons beaches, left, have safe bathing with places to stay right by the sea. To the north the **El Cotillo lighthouse beaches**, opposite page, have lots and lots of empty bays. It's surprising to see other people here, and astonishing if they're wearing anything

Hotel Playa Esmeralda
www.h10.es
esmeralda@h10.es
Tel: 00 34 928 87 53 53
Fax: 00 34 928 87 53 50
Thomson a la Carte, Airtours, First
Choice, Mundi Color

Sun River Club
www.hvsl.es (agent)
sunriver@hvsl.es
Tel: 00 34 928 54 72 94
Fax: 00 34 928 54 73 23
Airtours, Mundi Color, Medhotels.com

Hotel Sol Elite Gorriones
www.solmelia.es
sol.gorriones@solmelia.com
Tel: 00 34 928 54 70 25
Fax: 00 34 928 54 70 00
Thomson, Mundi Color

**Hotel Occidental Grand
Fuerteventura**
www.occidental-hoteles.com
reserves@oh-es.com
Tel: 00 34 928 87 36 00
Fax: 00 34 928 54 41 55
First Choice, Eclipse, Thomas Cook,
Airtours, Peng Travel

Hotel Club Jandia Princess
www.princess-hotels.com
Tel: 00 34 928 54 40 89
Fax: 00 34 928 54 40 97
Thomson, Mundi Color

Hotel Fuerteventura Princess
www.princess-hotels.com
Tel: 00 34 928 54 41 36
Fax: 00 34 928 54 41 37
Thomson

Monte Del Mar apartments
www.travellersway.co.uk
info@travellersway.co.uk
Tel: 00 34 928 54 40 88
Fax: 00 34 928 54 40 88
Travellers Way

Playa Esmeralda

On the outskirts of Costa Calma
A **pretty golden sand** beach on the sheltered side of the island which is popular for nude sunbathing and swimming. Sunbeds and umbrellas are available for hire.

From the centre of Costa Calma take the minor road south out of the township and fork left at the supermarket. The beach is 1 km further on, directly in front of the hotel.

Hotel Playa Esmeralda is a large 4-star establishment which opened in 2000. It is just above the nude beach and has superb views along the coast. The 4-star **Sun River Club** hotel at Costa Calma is set at the back of the resort about 1 km from the nearest beach, but has a nudist sun terrace on the roof.

Playa de Gorriones

Sotavento, 4 kms south of Costa Calma
A **wide flat beach** near the hotel of the same name, which stretches more than 20 kms south! There is a world-renowned windsurfing school here. The beach can be a bit exposed, but there are plenty of volcanic rock shelters.

Take the main **coast road south** from Costa Calma and after 3 kms watch for the sign to the Hotel Gorriones on the left. The road goes down to the beach.

The 4-star **Hotel Sol Elite Gorriones** is located on the beach with no other development nearby. It is a large well-equipped complex. The beach is clothes-optional within 100 metres of the hotel.

Playa Risco del Paso

Sotavento, 10 kms south of Costa Calma
Possibly the **finest beach on the island** with miles and miles of almost deserted golden sand. Fantastic sense of freedom for walking and relaxation dressed or undressed.

Take the **main road south** from Costa Calma and just before a large bend in the road and a filling station on the right there is a track on the left down to the beach. See the Playa Gorriones listing, above, for nearby hotels.

Playa Esquinzo

Butihondo, north of Morro Jable
This **beautiful clothes-optional beach** lies towards the southern end of the giant Playa de Sotavento. There is a selection of top-class hotels nearby.

Head **north from Morro Jable** along the main coast road.

Gain access by any of the large hotels here – all of the beaches next to them are clothes-optional and are open to all.

The **Hotel Occidental Grand Fuerteventura** is a 700-room, 4-star all-inclusive property that opened in May 2002. There is an extensive nudist area including a swimming pool, sunbathing lawns with loungers, open-air spa pool, turkish bath, sauna and vitamin bar. The 4-star **Hotel Club Jandia Princess** is set in extensive gardens. The beach is clothes-optional within a few steps of the property and the hotel sauna is nudist. Skinny-dippers frequently use a swimming pool next to the sauna, ignoring a small 'No FKK' (German for nudist) sign.

The **Hotel Fuerteventura Princess** is next to the Jandia Princess and opened in 2001. It shares the same bare beach as its older sister hotel. The **Monte Del Mar apartments** are built on an elevated site overlooking Playa Esquinzo, approximately 8 kms north of Morro del Jable. The beach below the apartments stretches for miles and is widely used by nude sunseekers.

Maravillosa beach

La Pared, Jandia

A **bracing beach** on the wild south-west coast of Fuerteventura, ideal for that exhilarating nude stroll or bare sunbathing in the shelter of one of the coves. Rough seas make swimming hazardous.

From Costa Calma take the **main road north** for 2 kms and look out for a left turn to La Pared. After 4 kms drive into the Hotel Costa Real car park and take the path by the side of the hotel on to the low cliffs, and then down the steps to the beach.

The 4-star **Hotel Costa Real** is situated on cliffs 300 metres from the sea. The hotel sauna and outdoor spa pool can be used nude. Rooms can be requested with a secluded terrace to allow private bare sunbathing.

El Cotillo surf beach is a great spot for seclusion but mind the undertow

1. **Playa Esmeralda**
2. **Playa de Gorriones**
3. **Playa Risco del Paso**
4. **Playa Esquinzo**
5. **Maravillosa beach**

Hotel Costa Real
www.chalfontholidays.co.uk
info@chalfontholidays.co.uk
Also: www.canariandreams.com
info@canariandreams.com
Tel: 00 34 928 54 90 04 (or 64)
Fax: 00 34 928 54 91 04
Travellers Way, Mundi Color, Chalfont Holidays, Canarian Dreams

Finca La Jaquita
www.teneriffa-urlaub.de
Email via website
Tel: 00 34 922 17 90 21
Canarian Dreams, Chalfont Holidays

Sotavento complex
www.chalfontholidays.co.uk
www.sotavento.es
info@chalfontholidays.co.uk
Tel: 01494 580728 (UK)
Chalfont Holidays

Red Rock beach, above and below, is a hugely popular spot for naked souls, partly because the island lacks sufficient bare beach opportunities. It's a must if you're visiting Tenerife. The island has plenty of hotels eager to answer the demand for bare bathing facilities, such as **Gran Hotel Costa Adeje**, below right, at Playa de las Americas

Tenerife

South coast

Red Rock beach

Playa la Tejita near El Medano

A beautiful **sheltered and secluded beach** ideal for swimming and sunning all year round. **Mount Teide**, Spain's highest peak, provides a stunning view. The beach is on the most southerly part of the island. Sun loungers are available for hire and there is a bar nearby. It's the most established and easily accessible bare beach on Tenerife, well used and well loved.

On the road from El Abrigo to El Medano there is a car park at the **eastern end of Playa la Tejita**. Walk towards the sea, keeping to the left until the bar at the end of the beach. There's a path behind the bar which takes you up and round a corner to a footbridge, and you're there – heaven!

El Medano is the closest town, and **Playa de las Americas** is 20 minutes' drive away. Accommodation is limited near the beach, but keen bare bathers could try the small naturist resort not far away. **Finca La Jaquita** has a selection of apartments and an attractive swimming pool set in tropical gardens. It's run like a family hotel and is five minutes' drive from Red Rock nude beach. It is even closer to La Paleda Playa (listed opposite).

Playa la Tejita

Near El Medano

This big open and **completely undeveloped beach** can best be described as clothes-optional. It has very dark-golden soft sand and is great for swimming. With lots of space it is easy to find a

quiet spot to yourself. **Dressed and undressed** sunseekers share the beach in harmony. It's sometimes breezy, in which case Red Rock (see above) around the corner at the eastern end of the bay might be a better bet.

The car park at the **eastern end** of the beach is ideal, and there is another one at the other end of the beach, towards El Abrigo.

As well as accommodation at **Finca La Jaquita** there is a privately owned apartment at the **Sotavento** complex, on the western side of the beach. It has two bedrooms, two bathrooms, a balcony and solarium suitable for au naturel sunbathing.

La Paleda Playa

Near El Medano

Very close to La Jaquita naturist resort and used by its residents, this small beach has **fine black volcanic sand** and is surrounded by low cliffs. Depending on the wind direction, it can be sheltered when Playa la Tejita is not. The beach slopes gently into the sea.

Take the local **coast road east** from El Medano for 2 kms. There is a car park at the end and a short easy walk down to the beach. **Finca La Jaquita** is a few hundred metres inland.

Playa de Puntillas

North of Playa de las Americas

An **attractive but remote** beach, 30-40 minutes brisk walk from civilisation. The lovely south-west facing shore with views to the island of La Gomera feels a million miles away from the brash hurly burly of nearby Playa de las Americas. Expect to find a few dozen other bare bathers and a handful of hippies who camp at the 200-metre long beach.

Approach on foot from the village of La Caleta taking the **well-trodden path** north climbing over two headlands or, from the village of El Puertito, head south along the coastal path. Take good footwear for this adventurous and **scenic hike**.

There are some new hotels at La Caleta, but for bare sunbathing at your hotel there's a great choice in Playa de las Americas, just 6 kms away. The 5-star **Gran Hotel Costa Adeje** has 457 rooms, an attractive rooftop terrace, pool and solarium with fine views and two secluded areas reserved for nude use. The 4-star **Hotel Fanabe Costa Sur** is just round the corner and also has a rooftop swimming pool and a big terrace, part of which is reserved for nude sunbathing.

The 4-star **Hotel Jardin Isla Bonita** has a nude solarium and splash pool on the roof, accessed by electronic room key.

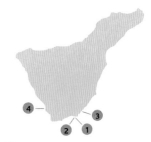

1. Red Rock beach
2. Playa la Tejita
3. La Paleda Playa
4. Playa de Puntillas

Gran Hotel Costa Adeje
www.costaadejegranhotel.com
info@costaadejegranhotel.com
Tel: 00 34 922 71 94 21
Fax: 00 34 922 71 56 56
Thomas Cook, Orchid Travel,
Medhotels.com, Euro-resorts.com

Hotel Fanabe Costa Sur
www.fanabecostasur.com
info@fanabecostasur.com
Tel: 00 34 922 71 29 00
Fax: 00 34 922 71 27 69
Thomson, Airtours, Thomas Cook,
Medhotels.com

Hotel Jardin Isla Bonita
www.hotelislabonita.com
info@hotelislabonita.com
Tel: 00 34 922 71 30 12
Fax: 00 34 922 71 24 92
JMC, Cosmos, Medhotels.com

1 Puerto de la Cruz

Mediterranean Palace and **Mare Nostrum Resort**
www.marenostrumresort.com
reservastfe@expogrupo.com
Tel: 00 34 922 75 75 00
Fax: 00 34 922 75 75 10
Sovereign, Thomas Cook, Cadogan, Mundi Color, JMC, Cosmos

Hotel Noelia Sur
www.dreamplacehotels.com
noeliasur@dphr.info
Tel: 00 34 922 79 35 11
Fax: 00 34 922 79 46 09
Airtours, Thomas Cook, Mundi Color, Euro-resorts.com

Puerto Palace
www.puertopalace.com
info@puertopalace.com
Tel: 00 34 922 37 24 60
Thomson, Mundi Color, Thomas Cook, Chalfont Holidays

Hotel Magec and Dania Park
www.daniamagec.com
info@daniamagec.com
Tel: 00 34 922 38 40 40
Thomson, Airtours, First Choice, Mundi Color, Chalfont Holidays

Parque Vacacional Eden Apartments
www.parquevacacionaleden.com
edenroc@jet.es
Tel: 00 34 922 38 05 00
Mundi Color

Maritim Hotel
www.maritim.de
info.ten@maritim.de
Tel: 00 34 922 37 90 00
Mundi Color, Millennium & Copthorne Hotels

The deluxe **Mediterranean Palace** has a lovely 'Adam and Eve' terrace with a swimming pool for skinny-dipping. The hotel is part of the **Mare Nostrum Resort** consisting of five 5-star hotels in the same complex, all offering access to the nude facilities. The other hotels are: Sir Anthony, Julio Cesar Palace, Cleopatra Palace and Marco Antonio Palace. The 4-star **Hotel Noelia Sur** is in town and a short walk from the beach. It has a secluded nudist terrace with panoramic views over the resort.

Tenerife north coast

While there are few bare beach opportunities in the north of Tenerife, nude sunbathing is readily available at a choice of hotels and apartments in the resort of **Puerto de la Cruz**.

The 4-star **Puerto Palace** has a lovely secluded rooftop swimming pool, spa pool, showers and terrace dedicated to nude relaxation and skinny dipping. The hotel is 1.5 kms from the town centre. A hard-to-get-to **naturist beach**, Playa de los Patos east of Bollulo, is 5 kms from the hotel, but the steep path requires considerable fitness and balance.

The 4-star **Hotel Magec** in the centre of Puerto de la Cruz has a nudist rooftop sun terrace on the ninth floor, sheltered by opaque glass. Guests at the **Dania Park** next door can also use the facilities at the Hotel Magec.

The **Parque Vacacional Eden Apartments** are set in three acres of gardens, with 216 studio and one-bedroom apartments. The complex has a secluded nudist sunbathing terrace and sauna. The 4-star **Maritim Hotel** at Los Realejos near Puerto de la Cruz has 296 rooms. It is set in extensive subtropical gardens, with a secluded nudist sunbathing lawn.

La Gomera

Playa del Ingles

Valle Gran Rey

A super volcanic **black sand beach** on the western side of this **subtropical island**, which has long been popular with bare bathers. The nude beach is an 800 metre walk to the north of the main promenade.

The **Las Tres Palmeras Apartments** by the sea at La Playa Calera, Valle Gran Rey, have been recently renovated. A footpath from the accommodation leads to the bare beach, which is just 400 metres away.

In this region, **Finca Argayall** is a holistic retreat 1 km south of **Vueltas** with home grown **organic produce** next to the sea. It specialises in all types of relaxation, meditation, massage and therapies such as Reiki and Shiatsu. Described as nude-friendly and the adjacent pebble beach is clothes-optional.

South coast

The popular 4-star **Hotel Jardin Tecina** at **Playa de Santiago** on the south coast is set in **extensive gardens** renowned for their flora and fauna. It is on the cliff top with a lift to the beach and has a nude sunbathing terrace on the roof as well as tennis and squash courts. There are three clothes-optional pebble bays within 20-40 mins walk east of the hotel.

Playa del Ingles, below, and **Finca Argayall**, left, are popular bare beach destinations on **La Gomera**. As with all the Canary islands, watch out for the fierce sun on your pale winter bottom – the wind is deceptively cooling – and take care in the Atlantic swell

1 **Playa del Ingles**
2 **Vueltas**
3 **Playa de Santiago**

Las Tres Palmeras Apartments
www.travellersway.co.uk
info@travellersway.co.uk
Tel: 00 34 922 80 57 93
Fax: 00 34 922 80 58 88
Travellers Way

Finca Argayall
www.argayall.com
Email via website
Tel/Fax: 00 34 922 69 70 08 or
Tel: 00 34 922 80 55 51
Book direct

Hotel Jardin Tecina
www.jardin-tecina.com
tecina@fredolsen.es
Tel: 00 34 922 14 58 50
Fax: 00 34 922 14 58 51
Thomson, Travellers Way, Sovereign, Real Spain, Airtours, Corona

Lanzarote

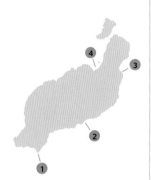

1 Playa Papagayo
2 Guasimeta and Matagorda
3 Charco del Palo
4 Playa Famara (listed p82)

South coast

Playa Papagayo

Near Playa Blanca

Not one but a collection of **beautiful and undeveloped** yellow sandy beaches in the natural park on the peninsula of the same name. All of the beaches are clothes-optional to some extent, but **Playa Caleta del Congrio** is the one most bare sunseekers head for. Over 500 metres long and ideal for walking and sunbathing. The beach is popular but there are no facilities, so take your own refreshments.

From Playa Blanca follow the signs to **Playa Papagayo**. After 2 kms pay a small toll to enter the **natural park**. After a further 1.5 kms along an unsurfaced road turn left at the sign to Playa Puerto Muelas. **Playa Caleta del Congrio** is the next beach on the right, on the eastern side of the peninsula. A large car park is nearby.

There is a wide choice of accommodation in Playa Blanca including three modern 4-star hotels that each have **nude sunbathing** terraces.

The **Iberostar Papagayo Hotel** on the outskirts of the resort at Playa de los Colorados opened in 2002. The au naturel terrace has super views. There is also a wellness centre and spa. The hotel helpfully advises there is an unofficial naturist area on the beach within five minutes' walk, to which they can direct customers.

The **Natura Palace Hotel** has a nude area in the garden. It also offers an extensive range of health and beauty treatments in its well-equipped spa. The **Timanfaya Palace Hotel** is popular and stylish, situated 2 kms to the west of the resort centre at Playa Flamingo. The bare sunbathing terrace is in a screened area of the **gardens**, and is furnished with sun-loungers and umbrellas.

Playa Guasimeta and Playa Matagorda

Near the airport between Arrecife and Puerto del Carmen

Two clean **sandy** clothes-optional beaches near to each other – Guasimeta is right alongside the runway at the airport, but is pleasant and feels, surprisingly, well away from civilisation. There are a couple of **beach bars** but it doesn't get too busy. Matagorda to the south has villas and other accommodation nearby. It's much more lively and you will probably find lots of

Iberostar Papagayo Hotel
www.iberostar.com
reservas@iberostar.com
Tel: 00 34 971 22 92 88
Fax: 00 34 971 71 65 35
Thomson, Mundi Color,
Medhotels.com

Natura Palace Hotel
www.hipotels.com
info@hipotels.com
Tel: 00 34 928 51 90 70
Fax: 00 34 928 51 90 75
Thomson, Portland, Mundi Color,
HVSL.es

Timanfaya Palace Hotel
www.h10.es
timan@h10.es
Tel: 00 34 928 51 76 76
Fax: 00 34 928 51 70 35
Thomson, Airtours, JMC, Mundi Color,
Sovereign, Cosmos

swimsuited beachbums as well as the happy bare ones. Both are good for swimming.

To get to Guasimeta take the turn for **Playa Honda** off the main road between the airport and Arricefe, and in less than 1 km you'll find a car park not far from the beach. Matagorda is by the saltflats on the **road from the airport** to Puerto del Carmen.

The 4-star **Hotel Los Jameos Playa** at Playa de los Pocillos is close to Matagorda and not too far from Guasimeta. There is a secluded area in its acres of tropical gardens reserved for nude sunbathing. Sunbeds with mattresses are provided as well as a freshwater shower. The hotel offers beauty treatments and has a sauna and gym.

North coast

Charco del Palo

Near Mala, between Costa Teguise and Arrieta
A unique **naturist village** by the sea that is **open to all**. There are plenty of sheltered and sandy spots for sunbathing

Hotel Los Jameos Playa
www.los-jameos-playa.de
losjameo@a1.web.es
Tel: 00 34 928 51 17 17
Fax: 00 34 928 51 42 19
Sovereign, Unijet, JMC Select, Mundi Color, Cosmos, Corona

Charco del Palo has a fabulous tidal swimming pool if you don't fancy braving the surf

Charco del Palo
www.charco-del-palo.com
charco@canariandreams.com
Tel: 0870 770 5378 (UK)
Fax: 0870 770 5379
Canarian Dreams

Charco Natural Apartments
www.charconatural.com
info@charconatural.com
Tel: 00 34 928 52 95 95
Fax: 00 34 928 52 95 95
Away with Dune

Las Piteras Apartments, Charco del Palo
www.laspiteras.es
info@laspiteras.es
Tel: 00 34 928 81 15 49
Fax: 00 34 928 80 04 67
Peng Travel

Villa Salida del Sol
www.salida-del-sol.de
Email via website
Tel: 00 49 5324 717 917
Fax: 00 49 5324 717 918
Book direct with owner

Hotel Playaverde
www.hotelesplaya.com
pverde@hotelesplaya.com
Tel: 00 34 928 59 06 09
Fax: 00 34 950 33 36 55 (central reservations)
Saga Holidays, Mundi Color, Hvsl.es

Famara holiday villas
www.famara.co.uk
info@canariandreams.com
Tel: 08707 705378 (UK)
Fax: 08707 705379
Canarian Dreams

Villa Vista Montana
www.islandseekers.co.uk
enquiry@islandseekers.co.uk
Tel: 01787 281417
Fax: 01787 281526
Island Seekers

and relaxing, but the beach is tiny and best for paddling. However, don't let that put you off because the coastline is beautiful and there is a large man-made **tidal swimming pool**, which is great fun. Or you can **swim in the sea** from steps on the rocks. There are miles of walks along the low cliffs above the Atlantic, where you can leave your clothes and your cares way behind you.

Travelling north, turn right off the coast road at the **village of Mala**, just after the small hospital. Follow the winding tarmac road for 3 kms until you reach Charco del Palo. You can be bare almost anywhere if you wish, and many of the holiday properties have lovely **skinny-dipping pools**.

There's a wide choice of accommodation at the naturist village, including luxury villas, bungalows and self-catering apartments. Also three restaurants, bars and a supermarket. The **Villa Salida del Sol** is a privately owned three-bedroomed villa overlooking the sea here. There are two bare terraces for all day sun.

The 4-star **Hotel Playaverde** at Costa Teguise is 15 minutes' drive from Charco del Palo. The hotel has a terrace reserved for all-over sunbathing.

Playa Famara

On the north-west coast (see map page 80)
The biggest beach on the island and certainly the **most dramatic**, backed by 2,000-foot cliffs! There's lots of space and the northern half is ideal for nude sunning, swimming and walking. The mini stone 'zocos', or shelters, provide protection from the breeze, as well as privacy for those who want it. The beach is popular with windsurfers.

Take the road from **Arrecife** to **Mozaga**, and then turn right for Teguise. After 3 kms turn left for **La Caleta** and Playa Famara. After 15 kms you can't miss the beach just before La Caleta.

There are one-, two- and three-bedroomed detached **holiday villas** immediately behind the beach and facing the sea. Some have secluded patios which are suitable for discreet nude sunbathing; the tour operator or website can advise. There are also plenty of privately owned apartments for hire in nearby **La Caleta**.

Villa Vista Montana is located in the countryside at Nazaret, a short distance from the coast. It has two bedrooms, two bathrooms and a large pool. With no close neighbours the sheltered terraces and pool are ideal for bare sunning and swimming. It is 15 minutes' drive from Charco del Palo naturist village and 20 minutes from Playa Famara.

Gran Canaria

Playa de Maspalomas

Close to Playa del Ingles on the southern tip of the island

Hundreds of acres of **sand dunes** that might have come straight from the Sahara frame the **beautiful long curved beach** between Maspalomas and Playa del Ingles. It's 3 kms from one end to the other and over 1 km deep. Along the shore it gets packed with holidaymakers, but there are specific places reserved for nude sunseekers. The bare areas, like the swimsuited ones, have sunbeds and umbrellas for hire. For a quieter spot, walk away from the sea into the vast expanse of dunes, but be careful not to get lost!

The best way on to the beach is from either end, although the **walk from Maspalomas** to the bare area is slightly shorter. Just look for the many other people without clothes.

The largest resorts on Gran Canaria have developed around this huge beach, so there is no shortage of places to stay. A number have nude sun terraces.

One novel aside is the restaurant **El Salvador** at Maspalomas, a large beach-side outdoor diner with a varied and reasonably priced menu. There is a secluded nude terrace on the first floor, overlooking Maspalomas beach and a short walk east from the bare section.

The 5-star **Hotel Palm Beach** at Maspalomas has a new health garden with saunas, steam rooms and a secluded nude terrace. The 4-star **Hotel IFA Dunamar** overlooking the sea at Playa del Ingles has been recently refurbished. There is a solarium with a naturist sunbathing area located on the roof.

The 4-star **Hotel Catarina** in Playa del Ingles has a solarium for bare relaxation on the roof. It is about 30 mins brisk walk or a short ride on the free shuttle bus to the beach. There is a 'Vitel' wellness centre that offers massage, acupuncture and homeopathy.

The 4-star **Sandy Beach Hotel** (details overleaf) in Playa del Ingles has a nude sundeck area on the roof. There is also a wellness centre offering yoga, health and beauty treatments, a gym and sauna.

1 Playa de Maspalomas

Hotel Palm Beach
www.hotel-palm-beach.com
info@hotel-palm-beach.com
Tel: 00 34 928 72 10 32
Fax: 00 34 928 14 18 08
Sovereign, Falcon Holidays, Thomas Cook Select, Classic Collections, Prestige Holidays, Hallmark, Whitehall Leisure

Hotel IFA Dunamar
www.ifacanarias.es
dunamar@ifacanarias.es
Tel: 00 34 928 77 28 00
Fax: 00 34 928 77 34 65
Sovereign, Eclipse, Thomson a la Carte, Mundi Color

Hotel Catarina
www.hvsl.es
hvpost@hvsl.es
Tel: 00 34 928 76 28 12
Airtours, Portland, Thomas Cook, Mundi Color, Direct Holidays

Ever-popular **Maspalomas**, below

Sandy Beach Hotel
www.sandy-beach.de
sandybea@a1web.es
Tel: 00 34 928 72 40 00
Fax: 00 34 928 72 40 08
Mundi Color, Euro-resorts.com

Hotel Gloria Palace
www.hotelgloriapalace.com
comercial@hotelgloriapalace.com
Tel: 00 34 928 12 85 00
Fax: 00 34 928 76 79 29
Mundi Color, Medhotels.com, Euro-resorts.com

IFA Beach Hotel
www.ifacanarias.es
dunamar@ifacanarias.es
Tel: 00 34 928 77 28 00
Fax: 00 34 928 77 34 65
Thomas Cook, Eclipse, Mundi Color

Helga Masthoff Park & Sport Hotel
www.helga-masthoff-hotel.com
h-masthoff-hotel@ctv.es
Tel: 00 34 928 14 21 00
HVSL agency (www.hvsl.es) or go direct

Magnolias Natura Bungalows
www.canariandreams.com
info@canariandreams.com
Tel: 0870 770 5378 (UK)
Fax: 0870 770 5379 (UK)
Canarian Dreams

The 4-star **Hotel Gloria Palace** overlooks the sea at San Agustin, next to Playa del Ingles. It has a panoramic nude sun terrace on the roof. The hotel thalassotherapy centre is claimed to be the largest of its kind in Europe.

The 3-star **IFA Beach Hotel** at San Agustin is located right on the edge of the dark golden sand. The company recently established a nudist sun terrace on the roof.

The 4-star **Helga Masthoff Park & Sport Hotel** is set in a rural location at Los Palmitos, about 15 minutes' drive from Maspalomas beach. There are six tennis courts, golf practice and pitch and putt. The wellness centre offers mud and seaweed beauty treatments and has a Finnish sauna, steam bath, spa pool and gym. There is a nudist sunbathing area. With just 47 rooms the atmosphere is relaxed and the food is good.

Close to Maspalomas beach and new for summer 2004 are the attractive **Magnolias Natura Bungalows**. The British owners have decided that in order to meet the growing demand from customers, the 28 units, the swimming pool and terraces will all be entirely clothes-optional. There is also a bar and restaurant. The bare accommodation is available from June 2004.

If you look at a map you'll see the Canaries are not that far from the Sahara desert. Walk into the dunes and you'll think you're actually there!

www.barebeaches.com

Balearic Islands

Balearic Islands

Sunny islands with deserted beaches are the very stuff of fantasy holidays. Given a bit of imagination, a willingness to explore, a determination to swim naked and a low-cost airline ticket – the Balearics are the place to make that fantasy come true.

One island in this group stands out as a firm favourite for all-over tan seekers. Formentera, close to the coast of Ibiza but a world away from the hubbub of its neighbour, has a selection of gorgeous bare-friendly beaches. It's a special place to visit, with a relaxed pace of life and clear blue sea lapping on the shore. A half-hour ferry ride from Ibiza is all it takes to find this bare beach heaven.

So saying, the three larger islands also have an astounding range of bare beaches. In Mallorca you can park your unclad bottom on a tiny nude cove with millionaires' yachts in the bay, or amble naked and alone along three miles of undeveloped sandy beach.

Ibiza, as we all know, attracts the party crowd so it's no surprise that the biggest nude beach on the island has a lively atmosphere. While on Menorca, there is a delightful family-friendly bare beach located on the south coast.

Formentera

Formentera is one of the most beautiful and welcoming places for bare bathing and only half an hour by fast ferry from its neighbour Ibiza. Almost every beach is a happy and peaceful mix of bare and clothed bathers, to a lesser degree during the busiest period of August and early September but even then you'll have no problem finding beaches for an all-over tan. In fact only one beach, Es Pujols, is considered no-go for nudity all year round. Many small and secluded beaches can be reached down tracks.

① Playa Illetas
② Playa Levante
③ Tanga beach

Playa Illetas, Levante and Tanga beach

Northern peninsula of Formentera

The two beautiful beaches of Illetas and Levante are back to back along a **thin peninsula** stretching to the north of the island. Both have **golden sands** and plenty of water sports on offer. Many, and often most, beach users are bare, and Levante is an official naturist beach. Illetas, on the west of the peninsula, and Levante are particularly handy for each other: if it's windy on one side it's just a **short stroll** to the calmer waters on the opposite beach. At the busiest times of the year most of the bare bathers go to Levante. And just south of Levante there is another popular clothes-optional bay called **Tanga beach**, which is nearer the tourist town of Pujols.

All the beaches on Formentera are **easy to find**. The island is small and you're never far from the coast. Simply park nearby and walk to the beaches.

One of the handiest places to stay for all these beaches is the 37-room **Hostal Sa Roqueta**, just north of Pujols and only 200 metres from Tanga beach.

Hostal Sa Roqueta
www.formentera-island.de/unterkuenfte
Tel: 00 34 971 32 85 06
Book direct

Formentera is a beach holiday paradise for bare and clothed visitors alike. The beaches and **blue waters** more than make up for the lack of other attractions

Insotel Club Formentera Playa
www.insotel.com
Tel: 00 34 971 32 80 00
Fax: 00 34 971 32 80 35
JMC Select, Thomson, Panorama, Sovereign

Hotel Riu Club La Mola
www.riu.com
Tel: 00 34 971 74 30 30
Thomson a la Carte, JMC Select, Sovereign

Talaya Bungalows
www.formentera.co.uk
enquiry@formentera.co.uk
Tel: 01642 210163 (UK)
Fax: 01642 222210 (UK)
Astbury Formentera

Playa Mitjorn has seen more and more people using it for bare bathing over the years

Playa Mitjorn

Formentera's long southern shore

These six miles of **largely undeveloped sandy bays** with rocky areas for snorkelling have tempted many people into their **first experience of bare bathing**. The beach is big enough for everyone and there are beach bars scattered along much of its length. The sea is more beautiful than the rocky coastline, and you can sit for hours gazing at the **brilliant blue waters**. It won't take any time to find groups of other bare bathers if you prefer comfort in numbers but nowadays the beach has mixed nude and dressed use – and some more deserted sections – for almost its entire length.

The beach is impossible to miss. It's much of the island's **southern coastline** and there are tracks leading to it from the island's main road.

There are a few hotel developments along this beach. The 4-star luxury **Insotel Club Formentera Playa** is in a quiet spot and you can lose your bikini after just a couple of minutes' walk along the beach. Another 4-star option is the **Hotel Riu Club La Mola**, again by the beach and just 5-10 minutes' walk from bare bathing. The **Talaya Bungalows** are set in attractive

gardens just 150m from clothes-free bliss – in fact some visitors don't go through the hassle of dressing simply for walking to the beach. Another good option is the **Pueblo Balear Casa Blanca**. This traditionally designed group of nine apartments is right by a quiet stretch of beach with a happy mix of clothed and dressed users – although most take the opportunity to strip off. Finally the **Hostal Ca Mari** is an attractive hostal in the middle of the beach just a few minutes from bare bathing.

Playa Es Calo

A short walk to the west of Es Calo town

This clothes-optional beach is a great alternative to the longer Playa Mitjorn on the other side of the island if it's windy there. Nudity is common for much of the year although less so during the peak season around August – Playa Mitjorn is within walking distance if you prefer. **Golden sand and rocks** for snorkelling, with a beach bar right at hand if you can bear to slip on your costume.

Simply walk for a few minutes along the shore to the left from **Es Calo town** past the harbour for fishing boats.

Good places to stay include the **Ses Platgetes** holiday bungalows, situated right on the beach, and **Miguel's apartment**, a penthouse flat above the owner's villa. It is just across the road from the beach.

Other beaches

Formentera has a famously relaxed attitude to bare bathing. Among other beaches used by nude and clothed visitors alike are **Cala Sahona** and much of the virtually uninhabited island **Espalmador**, just off the northern peninsula. Take care if wading across; the water reaches chest height.

1. Playa Mitjorn
2. Playa Es Calo
3. Cala Sahona
4. Espalmador island

Pueblo Balear Casa Blanca
www.formentera-app.com
info@formentera-app.com
Tel: 00 39 348 5167706 (Italy)
Fax: 00 34 971 32 86 05
Book directly with Italian owner
(in English)

Hostal Ca Mari
www.guiaformentera.com/camari
Tel: 00 34 971 32 81 80 and
00 34 971 32 82 83
Fax: 00 34 971 32 82 29
Book direct

**Ses Platgetes and
Miguel's apartment**
www.formentera.co.uk
enquiry@formentera.co.uk
Tel: 01642 210163 (UK)
Fax: 01642 222210 (UK)
Astbury Formentera

The beach at **Es Calo** has great sand but getting into the sea without sandals can be tricky

① Playa Es Trenc
② Playa Es Pregons Gran

Mallorca

Playa Es Trenc

Near Colonia Sant Jordi, south-east Mallorca
The best known and one of the **prettiest bare beaches** on the island. It has a long undeveloped shoreline with lovely soft yellow sand. The beach shelves gently into the turquoise sea – perfect for swimming. Low **dunes and pinewoods** complete this beautiful spot.

There are sunbeds and umbrellas for hire on part of the nude section, or for more tranquillity just walk a little further. As bare bathing becomes a commonplace activity for holidaymakers visitor numbers inevitably rise, but secluded beaches like this still have plenty of space.

Take the lanes to the seaside hamlet of **Ses Covetes**. On entering the village look out for a left turn into a wide unmade track by the phone box. Arrive early and park here, otherwise there is a large car park (with charge) just before the village. Walk 200 metres along the track to the start of the beach, then another 300 metres to the nude area.

Many holidaymakers stay in **Colonia Sant Jordi**, from where it is possible to walk along the beach to the southern, clothes-optional, end of Es Trenc.

Playa Es Pregons Gran

Colonia Sant Jordi, south-east Mallorca
This wonderful little bare bay has a crescent of **fine yellow sand** 180 metres long. The sea is transparent and looks more like the Caribbean – a paradise for 'kids' of all ages. There are no beach bars so bring your picnic and **plenty of drinks**. In our opinion, the **jewel in the crown** of the Es Trenc area.

The route to the beach is a pleasant 15 minute walk along the shore, heading north from **Colonia**. Start at the Hotel Marques Del Palmer, and it's the third bay along. The fourth bay, if you walk further, is the southern end of the main Es Trenc beach.

The Swiss-owned 4-star **Hotel Marques Del Palmer** is in a lovely location at the water's edge on the outskirts of town. The hotel is adjacent to the attractive Playa es Marques, sometimes described as Estanys Playa.

The **Villa Piccola Apartments** in Colonia is a small privately owned luxury development (4 keys), located opposite the Hotel Marques Del Palmer. The accommodation enjoys similar access to the stunning nude beaches of Pregons Gran and Es Trenc.

Villa Marquesa Apartments in Colonia provide basic

Hotel Marques Del Palmer
www.universaltravel.ch
marques@universalhotels.org
Tel: 00 34 971 65 51 00
Fax: 00 34 971 65 63 69
Universal Travel (Switzerland)

Villa Piccola Apartments
www.baleares.com/fincas/piccolaing.htm
info@villapiccola.com
Tel: 00 34 971 65 60 93
Fax: 00 34 971 65 60 33
Davimar Tours (Mallorca),
Agroturismo Balear (Mallorca)

Villa Marquesa Apartments
Tel: 00 34 971 65 51 00
Fax: 00 34 971 65 63 69
Book via Hotel Marques Del Palmer
(same tel and fax numbers)

The long **Playa Es Trenc**, opposite, is tempting more and more people to cast off their costumes – but it still has plenty of space for all. Picture courtesy the Balearic tourist board

1. Playa El Mago
2. Playa Son Real
3. Cala Mesquida

Hotel El Coto
hotelcoto@navegalia.com
Tel: 00 34 971 65 50 25
Fax: 00 34 971 65 50 01
Book direct

Hotel Sur Mallorca
www.hsurmallorca.com
surmallorca@hoteleraalfa.es
Tel: 00 34 971 65 52 00
Fax: 00 34 971 65 53 00
Book direct

Hotel Son Baulo
www.fehm.es
hotelsonbaulo@teleline.es
Tel: 00 34 971 85 01 14
Fax: 00 34 971 85 18 17
Thomson

Hotel Prinsotel La Pineda
www.prinsotel.es/pineda.htm
pineda@prinsotel.es
Tel: 00 34 971 56 46 84
Fax: 00 34 971 56 55 36
Interhotel.com

holiday accommodation (1 key) situated next door to Villa Piccola and only one minute longer to walk to the naturist beaches. The modern 4-star **Hotel El Coto** in Colonia is near Playa es Marques beach and a 900-metre walk from Pregons Grans bare beach.

The 3-star high-rise **Hotel Sur Mallorca** in Colonia is built on a rocky peninsula with the sea on three sides. Although across town from the bare beaches, it's good value. Request a south-west facing room on the top floor for fantastic views.

Playa El Mago

Near Portals Vells, south-west Mallorca

This delightful and picturesque little cove must be the **smallest official nudist beach in Spain**. It has soft golden sand and calm sheltered water ideal for swimming and snorkelling. However, it gets **extremely busy** and bare and swimsuited sunbathers spread out on the smooth rocks surrounding the bay. There is a restaurant.

Drive south from **Magaluf** towards **Portals Vells**, past the golf course and into the pinewoods. Take the left turn signposted Playa de Mago Restaurant.

Playa Son Real

Near C'an Picafort, north Mallorca

A string of **protected and undeveloped** clothing-optional beaches stretching for 2 kms to the east of the main resort, which attract both bare and swimsuited users. Driftwood and occasional seaweed help make this part of the coast feel remote. There are no facilities so remember to take refreshments with you.

From C'an Picafort walk out of town along the beach past the last property, **Hotel Son Baulo**, and the shore is yours to bare within 350 metres. Or drive to **Son Serra Nou** and walk west towards C'an Picafort. A second wild and remote nude beach can be found by walking east from Son Serra village.

Cala Mesquida

North-east Mallorca, near Cala Ratjada

A **beautiful white sand** beach with good facilities and **superb swimming**. The area is developing rapidly with apartments and hotels, so the beach is very popular. Bare bathers tend to use the southern side of the bay, near the pill box. Turn off the Arta to Cala Ratjada road at **Capdepera**, following the signs to Cala Mesquida. Park by the holiday village and take the path to the beach.

The 3-star **Hotel Prinsotel La Pineda** at Cala Ratjada has 350 rooms and apartments. Located 600 metres from Cala Guya beach and 500 metres from the port of Cala Ratjada. Not one but **two nudist sun terraces** on the roofs of buildings 4 and 6. The hotel is 8 kms from the bare beach at Cala Mesquida.

Menorca

Playa Son Bou

St Jaime, south Menorca
The biggest sandy beach on the island, with a long tradition of bare bathing. It **shelves gently** into the sea and is **super for children**. There are plenty of facilities on this busy **blue flag**

1 Playa Son Bou

Playa Son Bou has a long and noble tradition of bare bathing. Picture from the Balearic tourist board

beach. The established nude area is on the western side of the bay, away from the two large hotels.

Travelling along the main road from Mahon towards Ciutadella, turn left to **St Jaime**, just after the town of **Alayor**. In 6 kms park by the beach.

You can't miss the twin high-rise family hotels **Sol Milanos** and **Sol Pinguinos**, built right by Son Bou beach. They are both 3-star and have a total of 600 rooms.

According to one brochure 'clothing requirements descend from the start of the hotels where bikinis and shorts are required, to the end stretch of the beach which is **au naturel**'. In other words the further you go the better it gets, only 10-15 mins walk at most.

Cala Macarelleta

Cala Macarella, south-west Menorca

A **picture-postcard cove** which is completely unspoilt and has warm clear water lapping on the soft white sand. Surrounded by **pinewoods and rocky headlands**, this secluded inlet is particularly sheltered. Popular with visiting yachts, there is sometimes a mix of swimsuited and bare bathers.

Drive through the lanes south-east from **Ciutadella to Cala Macarella** – the last 4 kms are bumpy. Walk from the car park and turn right (facing the sea). Scramble over the **headland** to the next bay, Cala Macareletta. It is not difficult, but not for the infirm.

Ibiza

Playa de Es Cavallet

Near the southernmost tip of Ibiza

A long sandy bare beach which is especially popular with **young people and partygoers**, though there is plenty of space for all on this official nude beach. It stretches for more than 1 km. Well equipped with **bars, sunbeds and umbrellas**. Always a lively cosmopolitan atmosphere, there is something here for everybody.

Travel south from Ibiza town, passing **Playa den Bossa** and the salt pans. The beach is signposted and there is a car park. There are buses from town; alternatively it's a pleasant cycle ride.

Aguas Blancas Beach

Figueral, north-east Ibiza

A string of pretty light sandy beaches with calm clear turquoise

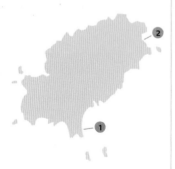

www.barebeaches.com

water. Backed by clay cliffs, often used for **plastering on bare bodies** as a skin tonic. These shores are officially nudist and very relaxed. There is a good beach bar nearby. A slight drawback out of season – some of the beaches **lose the sun** later on because of the cliffs, so get there in good time if you want to make the most of your day.

Travel 1 km north from **Figueral** and there is a choice of rough parking areas on the descent to the sea. From the beach bar turn left (facing the sea) for the au naturel coves.

The informal 30-room **Hostal Sa Plana**, near Playa de Figueral, is surrounded by pine-clad hills and located 15 minutes' walk from the nude beach at Aguas Blancas.

Hostal Sa Plana
www.ibiza-hotels.com/saplana
saplana@caeb.net
Tel: 00 34 971 33 50 73
Fax: 00 34 971 33 55 51
Book direct

Aguas Blancas: if you fancy a spot of natural body painting, the clay from the cliffs works wonders. And if your partner's reluctant just tell them it's good for the skin. Picture courtesy the Balearic tourist board

Save your skin

Sunlight is vital to the body's physical and mental wellbeing. It stimulates our natural production of **vitamin D** and without it, we can feel tired and depressed. It is thought that sunshine helps the release of endorphins and other 'feel good' chemicals in the body, which help to repair and engage the body in **wellbeing and long-term health**.

But to enjoy fully the freedom and hedonism of **sunbathing naked**, it is essential to protect your body from the sun's harmful rays. When we step out into the sunshine for the first time, most of us can withstand the sun's rays without any sun protection for a **maximum of 20 minutes** before burning.

So you need to choose a suitable sun cream that offers the correct **European sun protection factor** (SPF) for your skin type. For example, if you choose a sun cream with SPF 8, you have protection that allows you to stay in the sun eight times longer than you could without protection, before burning. However, it is important to remember that if you are sunbathing nude for the first time, you must also be very careful to adequately protect **newly exposed areas of the skin**, like your bottom and breasts. If you're used to going bare, they tan like any other part of the body.

Remember also to stay out of the sun between 12 noon and 2pm when the **sun is at its hottest** and wear a sun hat if you are prone to heat stroke. No need to get dressed otherwise though, sitting in the shade on a warm day is lovely without a stitch on.

Finally, you can help to boost your body's reaction against skin damage by taking supplements. **Vitamin C** is an effective antioxidant while **vitamin E** can act as a natural sunscreen. The mineral **selenium** has also been found to be effective in preventing sunburn, while **zinc** is an effective treatment for minor burns and skin complaints. But bear in mind that there is no substitute for regularly applying sun cream with the correct SPF for your skin type and for looking after your bare body.

Greek islands

Greek islands

A favourite destination for lovers of pure relaxation in this beautiful laid back Mediterranean region. Island hopping is easy and a popular way to visit lots of different places, and lots of bare beaches. An array of historic sights – Knossos on Crete is particularly inspiring – provide added attractions. Accommodation ranges from simple to sophisticated, but the Greeks are always warm and friendly.

There are surprisingly few places where nude sunbathing is officially approved, but it's very popular, and the local tourist office is always happy to offer directions to the nearest clothes-optional beach. Generally, the best nude places can be found out of town on the less crowded parts of the coast.

Corfu, Kefalonia, Skiathos, Skopelos, Mykonos, Rhodes and Crete are just some of the islands of interest to travellers who enjoy bathing in their birthday suits. You will certainly find plenty of other like-minded souls.

For more bare beaches in Greece, look at:
www.geocities.com/hotsprings/1794
www.gogreece.about.com/cs/nudebeaches

Crete

This wonderful island has the seclusion and beauty that make being naked on the beach a heavenly way to feel at one with nature. It is a great place whether you're a **shy first-timer** or a **life-long enthusiast**. The most popular bare beaches in Crete are on the south coast. It even has a friendly naturist hotel if you want to indulge in a truly **stress-free holiday**. There are many bare beaches; we've selected some of the better known but more can be found on the helpful Cap'n Barefoot website www.geocities.com/hotsprings/1794/crete/crete.html

① Sweetwater beach

Sweetwater beach

Between Loutro and Chora Sfakion
A dramatic cliff backdrop and **beautiful clear water** are two of this beach's best features. The beach is smooth pebbles and takes its name from freshwater wells at the back. A taverna built on a platform in the sea makes a useful – and pretty – addition to the beach, which has little natural shade. It's a great place to get a tan and almost all visitors go bare.

From Chora Sfakion town take the **coast road west** to Anapolis. Soon after Ilingas beach the road takes a sharp right bend back on itself to zig-zag up the mountain. Take the **coastal footpath** at the bend (marked E4) to continue along the shore. The beach is 30-45 minutes' walk along a rocky path above the sea. The path then leads on to the coastal village of Loutro, about 45 minutes away. Alternatively take a **15-minute ferry ride** from Chora Sfakion.

Sweetwater beach is a spectacular and remote spot. The fact you can skinny dip here has pleasantly surprised many a warm walker using the coastal path running along the back of the beach

Vritomartis Hotel and Bungalows
www.naturism-crete.com
vritnat@otenet.gr
Tel: 00 30 28250 91112
Away With Dune, Canarian Dreams,
Chalfont Holidays

Fata Morgana Apartments
www.fatamorgana-kreta.com
info@fatamorgana-kreta.com
Tel: 00 30 28250 92077
Simply Greece

Filaki beach, below, is handy for the lovely **Hotel Vritomartis**, the only naturist hotel in Crete. Picture courtesy of the hotel

Filaki beach

Chora Sfakion town

A beautiful **pebble beach** just outside the town of Chora Sfakion. The beach is used by the nearby naturist hotel Vritomartis and is open to all bare beach lovers. The hotel runs a beach bar and there are sunbeds and parasols for hire. A beautiful bay for naked **bathing and snorkelling**.

The beach is 900 metres from Hotel Vritomartis. As you drive into Chora Sfakion, the hotel is on the left about 500 metres before the main town. From this street a lane on the left goes to the beach.

Vritomartis Hotel and Bungalows is a good quality 3-star family-owned hotel. Its pool and outside areas are all nude during the day and the hotel has a free, regular minibus to Filaki beach. There are 85 rooms, half in the main hotel and half in bungalows set in extensive grounds. A lovely place ideal for all bare souls, not just the keener naturist visitor.

Frangokastello beach

By the town of Frangokastello

The town is worth visiting for both its **dramatic coastal castle** and its big sandy nude beach. The sea is gently shelving so is

great for families, and at the very end are clay pebbles under a waterfall if you fancy some **natural bodypainting**.

The beach to the east of the town (to the left as you face the sea) is used for nude bathing. To drive there head east from Frangokastello and after 500 metres turn right down the track marked Sunrise Taverna. Park and walk down the steps then walk to the left.

Fata Morgana Apartments is a modern development and taverna situated directly above the beach. To get to the nude beach it's a short climb down to the sand and then a walk to the left from the apartments.

Plakias beach

Plakias town

A fabulous setting of cliffs, mountains and a **huge sweep of golden sand** make this beach a wonderful place for all-over tanning and fine snorkelling. The sea shelves gently, making it suitable for families, and there are showers available. **Refreshments** are brought to the beach in season, and umbrellas are also available.

The nude area is the last section of the beach, to the left as you

1. Filaki beach
2. Frangokastello beach
3. Plakias beach

Frangokastello beach, below, is gently shelving for safer bathing and is a handy place to take a break from sightseeing in the town

Plakias Bay Hotel
www.c-v.net/hotel/plakias/plakiasbay
plbay@otenet.gr
Tel: 00 30 8320 31215 and 31315
Zorbastravel.gr

Europe's bare bottom: Crete and its tiny sister island of Gavdos are the most southerly point in Europe, making **Agios Pavlos** beach, above, one of the continent's most southerly nude beaches. **Micro Amoudi** beach along the coast, below, is well loved by nude beach enthusiasts

face the sea, and unsurprisingly it is often the most popular part of the whole bay.

Plakias Bay Hotel has 28 apartments, a reputation for good food, and is just three minutes walk from the bare beach area.

Micro Amoudi

By Damnoni beach
This is in fact two **sandy bays**, set between the much larger Damnoni and Amoudi beaches on either side. Sunbeds, parasols and a **cold shower** are available in the larger of the two bays (on the west or right as you face the sea). The smaller bay is therefore usually quieter, particularly as it involves a slightly tricky climb down. The beaches are popular, friendly, and often there's not even a single swimming costume in sight.

The bays are **easy to find and reach**. From Amoudi you go right as you face the sea, taking a short path uphill to take you into the nude bay. From Damnoni you go left along a track that's also suitable for vehicles if you're in a hurry to get undressed.

Plakias Bay Hotel is a long walk or short drive away (see details under Plakias beach, above).

The Red Beach

Matala town

A famous and popular place for baring all and one of the Travel Channel's **top 10 nude beaches** in the world. Most of the bathers usually enjoy this sandy beach naked. Don't rely on finding refreshments for sale as facilities here vary from season to season.

On arrival in Matala take the **left hand road** immediately after the Hotel Zafirias. The sealed road gives way to a track which takes you to the beach. When you come to a fence go through the gate and down to the beach. **Ferries** are also available from Matala town.

Agios Pavlos

At the **lovely little village** of Agios Pavlos, worth visiting just for the views, there is a long-established nude beach over the headland. The walk down to the beach is a fairly steep sandy slope that gets hot in the sun. There is plenty of room for peace and quiet while you sunbathe and swim. A heavenly and **secluded spot** with fine views along the coast.

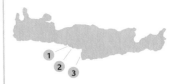

1. Micro Amoudi
2. Agios Pavlos
3. The Red Beach

Agios Pavlos is a fabulous spot with a sandy beach, beautiful views and plenty of space for everyone

① Sougia

Sougia, below and bottom right, has a convenient bare beach right by the unspoilt town, making it popular with discerning travellers looking to mix skinny-dipping into their trip. Pictures courtesy www.sougia.info. **Micro Amoudi**, opposite top, is used almost exclusively by bare bathers – ordinary beaches lie on either side of it for swimsuit wearers

The bare beach is easy to find. Facing the bay at Agios Pavlos, walk over the **headland** on your right and down to the beach on the other side.

Sougia

East of Sougia town

This beautiful beach could not be easier to find. Bare bathing is popular and commonplace **immediately to the east** of the built-up area in Sougia town. The water is excellent for swimming and snorkelling, with safe **natural rock pools** for children. The beach is small pebbles, fine enough to make it comfortable for sunbathing. There is a happy mix of dress and undress on the beach, although the nude bathers often comfortably outnumber the clothed ones. Sougia is highly regarded among bare beach lovers as a largely **unspoilt town** in a beautiful part of the island. Further to the east, beyond a rock, is a more **secluded area** with springs and caves to explore. Tourist info, accommodation and much else of use to the visitor is available in English from www.sougia.info

Nude bathing starts at the very edge of the town: this beach is unmissable in every sense if you're staying in Sougia.

① **Myrtiotissa beach**

Villa Myrto
www.villamyrto.com
ralitaki@otenet.gr
Tel: 00 30 2661 09 50 82
Book through 'Wish I Was There'
www.cbaltd.demon.co.uk/c-bits

Villa Kapella
www.corfu-villas-apts.com
korfuapps@otenet.gr
Tel: 00 30 2661 09 45 63
Fax: 00 30 2661 08 02 60
Book direct

Villa Atraides
www.villa-atraides.com
info@villa-atraides.com
Tel: 00 30 2661 08 02 44
Fax: 00 30 2661 08 02 44
Book direct

① West Xi beach

Kefalonia Palace Hotel
www.all-hotels-greece.com
Tel: 00 30 26710 92555
Thomson, JMC, Airtours, Amathus,
Olympic, Portland

Corfu

Myrtiotissa beach

Near Pelekas, on the west coast
A beautiful bare beach with a **freshwater spring** tumbling off the tree-covered cliffs. A favourite place of writer **Lawrence Durrell**. Sunbeds and traditional Greek refreshments available. Although the track from the car park is very steep you will find plenty of like-minded company, both swimsuited and au naturel. Swimming and snorkelling are excellent. Bare bathers tend to use the south side of the bay.

Local information is available from www.myrtiotissa.com

Take the road from **Vatos to Glyfada** and turn right immediately after Villa Myrto. Drive into the car park among the trees and walk down to the beach.

Villa Myrto, a family run property, has self-catering apartments set in olive and lemon groves. Myrtiotissa beach is a 10-minute walk. **Villa Kapella** at Vatos has good value self-catering studios and apartments 1.5 kms from Myrtiotissa bare beach.

Villa Atraides near Pelekas has four double en-suite letting rooms and is for adults only. It has good views over the surrounding countryside and costumes are optional for sunbathing and swimming in the large pool. It is 10 minutes' drive from Myrtiotissa.

Kefalonia

West Xi beach

Lixouri, at the southern end of the Paliki peninsula
A lovely bare beach of reddish-orange sand more than 1 km long, which is **completely undeveloped** – it's unspoilt but there are no sunbeds or tavernas. Backed by clay cliffs, you may well have this sheltered haven more or less to yourself. The swimming is excellent but remember to take your own sunshade and refreshments.

Drive **south from Lixouri** towards the western end of the main Xi beach. Park and continue west on foot over a small hill to the bare beach. Local info is available from kefhelm.tripod.com, which lists more bare beaches.

The 4-star **Kefalonia Palace Hotel** is relatively isolated at the western end of the main Xi beach. In low season there is some clothes-optional bathing on the adjacent beach to the east, while the bare beach itself is reached by a path over the small hill to the west.

Skiathos

Banana beach

Near Koukounaries, on the south-west coast

Banana beach is the collective name for three lovely sandy bays well known by nude bathers. The water is **crystal clear** and normally perfectly calm. Each of the owners that run the three small tavernas looks after the beaches and ensures they are kept spotless. During peak season bare beachbums may feel more comfortable on **Little Banana**, one of the smaller coves, as large numbers of clothed holidaymakers descend on the main beach. Little Banana is often described as the **best bare beach in Greece**, although there is plenty of competition for the accolade. Local info is available from www.sunnybanana.com

There is a bus turnaround and car park at the end of the **Koukounaries road**, coming from Skiathos town. The track to Big Banana is signposted and takes 15 mins walking through the **olive groves**. From here it's only 5-10 mins to Little Banana.

There is plenty of accommodation served by UK tour operators. The **Golden Beach** family-run hotel is one of the nearest to Banana at 15-20 mins walk. The **Muses Hotel** at Koukounaries is a 'B' category property 20 mins walk from Banana. The 'B' category **Caravos Hotel Resort** at Koukounaries is within easy walking distance of six attractive beaches, including the Banana beaches.

The self-catering **Periyali Studios** are on a hillside 200 metres from the Golden Beach hotel, where guests can use the swimming pool, and is just over 15 mins' brisk walk from Banana. **Maria Villa and Studios** consists of a two-bedroom villa for four people and three studios for two people each. The complex is 15-20 mins walk from Banana.

① **Banana and Little Banana**

Banana beach takes its name from the fact it's yellow and curved like a banana. Bare bathers tend to gather at **Little Banana** rather than the main beach, above. Both pictures courtesy of www.sunnybanana.com

The Golden Beach
www.libraholidays.co.uk
info@libraholidays.co.uk
Tel: 00 30 2427 04 93 95
First Choice, Libra, Thomson Small
and Friendly, Argo, Olympic

Muses Hotel
www.libraholidays.co.uk
info@libraholidays.co.uk
Libra Holidays, First Choice,
Argo Holidays

Caravos Hotel Resort
www.caravos.com
caravos@can.gr
Tel: 00 30 2427 04 94 45
Fax: 00 30 2427 04 93 81
First Choice, Unijet, JMC, Argo
Holidays, Libra, Olympic

Periyali Studios
www.argo-holidays.com
Argo Holidays

Maria Villa and Studios
www.travelalacarte.co.uk
info@travelalacarte.co.uk
Tel: 01635 863 030 (UK)
Travel a la Carte

① **Velanio beach**

Hotel Ostria
www.skopelos.net/ostria
ostria20@otenet.gr
Tel: 00 30 24240 22220
Fax: 00 30 24240 23236
Book direct

Poseidon Villas
www.skopelos.net/poseidon
poseidon_villas@yahoo.com
Tel: 00 30 24240 24153
Fax: 00 30 24240 24374
Book direct

Paradise Camping
www.paradise-greece.com
reception@paradisemykonos.com
Tel: 00 30 22890 22852
Fax: 00 30 22890 24350
Book direct

Hotel Argo
www.mykonos-accommodation.com
argo-hotel@mykonos-
              accommodation.com
Tel: 00 30 22890 23160
Fax: 00 30 02890 24137
Libra Holidays

Skopelos

Velanio beach

Staphylos, on the south coast

A super bare bay consisting of sand and fine shingle, described by Skopelas Tourist Board as '**the beach of the nudist**'. Surrounded by picturesque **natural countryside**, this unspoilt shore is a favourite haunt for all-over tan seekers. Most nudes tend to use the area beyond the rocky outcrops. Swimming is delightful.

Travel south from Skopelos town for 4 kms to Staphylos. Park or alight from the bus near the Hotel Ostria. Walk down to Staphylos bay and at the other end of the beach simply walk over the headland to Velanio. Tourist info from www.skopelosweb.gr

The 'B' category and family-run **Hotel Ostria** overlooks Staphylos beach. It is 750 metres from Velanio bare beach. The **Poseidon Villas** consist of maisonettes and flats located opposite the Hotel Ostria. Guests can use the swimming pool at the hotel. It's 750 metres from Velanio.

Mykonos

Paradise and Super Paradise

Near Platis Yialos, on the south coast

These are two of the most famous bare beaches in the Aegean and even the Mediterranean. They traditionally attract a young, **lively cosmopolitan crowd**. During peak season there is a real party atmosphere – music included! Perhaps more fairly described as 'clothes-optional' these days, because there's likely to be a relaxed mix of dressed and undressed visitors. Super Paradise is also very popular with **gay holiday makers**. Refreshments are available at both locations and the swimming is superb.

The beaches are well signposted and served by buses from Mykonos town. Another popular way to travel in summer is by the **traditional small boats** (caiques) that shuttle backwards and forwards from nearby Platis Yialos.

Paradise Camping offers a range of accommodation to suit all budgets, including apartments, rooms, beach cabins and tents. Expect to find the **clubbing set** in residence – no early nights here.

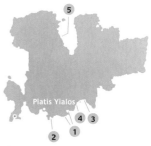

Hotel Argo, a family establishment in Platis Yialos, offers a quieter base, 4 kms from Mykonos town. It is just 100 metres from the beach where regular caiques call at the pier to ferry passengers to Paradise and Super Paradise.

Other south coast beaches

In addition to the Paradise beaches there are three more bays on the southern coast where people often go bare. They are also accessible by boat from Platis Yialos. **Paranga beach** is the next bay going east, before Paradise. Then there's **Elia beach**, which is the furthest east the boats go, beyond Super Paradise. **Agrari beach** is a short walk back to the west from Elia.

1. Paradise and Super Paradise
2. Paranga
3. Elia
4. Agrari
5. Panormos

Panormos beach

North-east from Mykonos town
A delightful and less busy bare beach on Panormos bay. There are **two tavernas** at one end of the beach, buff bathing is the norm at the other end. Can be **breezy** if the prevailing north wind blows.

From Mykonos town drive **north-east** across the island, following the signs to Panormos beach.

The category 'A' **Albatros Club Hotel** at Panormos provides the only holiday accommodation. The bare area is just a walk along the beach.

Albatros Club Hotel
www.united-hellas.com/tourism/
mykonos/albatros
Tel: 00 30 22890 25130 or
00 30 22890 27230
Fax: 00 30 22890 25361
Book direct

Paros

Lageri beach

Across the bay from Naousa, to the north-east tip of the island
A long narrow **golden sand** bare beach considered by some to be **heaven on earth**. Completely undeveloped – no tavernas or even any roads nearby. The water is crystal clear, the sand is soft underfoot and the land behind the shore is covered in beautiful flora. Towards the **southern end of the beach** is best for au naturel sunseekers.

Small boats that go regularly from Naousa are by far the favoured way to get to the beach, due to the **lack of roads**. It is possible to drive part of the way, travelling east from town towards Santa Maria, and then walk the remainder.

Naousa itself is described as the **pearl of Paros**, full of historical antiquities, archaeological monuments and famous places such as the Acropolis of Koukounaries.

For accommodation, try **Sakis Rooms**; in a quiet elevated

1. Lageri

Sakis Rooms
www.paros-online.com
info@paros-online.com
Local info: www.parosweb.gr

① **Porto Paros**
② **Monastiri**

Porto Paros
www.atlantis.gr/porto-paros
porto-paros@atlantis.gr
Tel: 00 30 22840 52010
Fax: 00 30 22840 51720
Book direct

location overlooking a nearby beach and three minutes from town. They have an informative website.

Porto Paros beach

Across the bay from Naousa, on the north of the island
A small crescent of **fine golden sand** that is clothes-optional. Only 80 metres long and 7 metres wide, it attracts anything up to 30 sunbathers, mostly nude. It is lovely and clean and there are no facilities other than waste bins. Easy to get to.

Take the **road from Naousa** towards Monastiri, and just past the Porto Paros Hotel there is a short footpath down to the beach. Alternatively, use a taxi boat from Naousa to Porto Paros, by the aqua park, and walk north for 300 metres.

The 4-star **Porto Paros** hotel has 130 rooms and 70 apartments and is on the western side of the Gulf of Naousa.

Monastiri

Agios Ioannis, near the northern tip of the island
There are lots of attractive **little remote coves** to explore in the area, mostly suitable for bare bathing and even bare walking. There are no facilities or shade and the surrounding area is isolated – escapist territory!

Again, the top of the peninsula can be reached by boat from **Naousa**, or by driving up the western side of the gulf, signposted from town.

Antiparos

Theologians nudist beach

Just outside and to the north of Antiparos village
This popular beach is unusual because it is one of the very few **'official' nudist beaches** in Greece, and has been since the early 1970s. Although the sandy shoreline is less than 100 metres long, it is possible to carry on to the next beach. You can also go bare if you wade to the small offshore **island of Diplo**. Lots of opportunity for bare exploration and if it's windy there are dunes at the back of the beach for shelter. **Refreshments** and a **mini-market** are available at the nearby campsite.

The nudist beach is **700 metres walk** north from the harbour in Antiparos village. Local information is available from www.antiparos-isl.gr

Camping Antiparos just west of the nudist beach offers plenty of space for tents. There are also bamboo huts for hire.

① **Theologians nudist beach**
② **Diplo island**

Camping Antiparos
www.antiparos-isl.gr/campingantiparos
kalargyros@par.forthnet.gr
Tel/Fax: 00 30 22840 61221

Lesvos

Molyvos Delphinia beach

Between Molyvos and Petra, on the north-west coast

This pleasant **coarse-sand** bare beach is close to the Delphinia Hotel. It is quiet and has a **handful of sunbeds** and umbrellas, but no other facilities. Swimming is good. There are great views of Molyvos town along the coast.

From Molyvos travel south towards Petra for just over 3 kms and look for Hotel Delphinia. There is a **track** down the side of the hotel signposted to the beach. At the beach turn left and walk to the end section.

The **Delphinia Hotel and Bungalows** resort is set in 87 acres of parkland by the sea. The au naturel area of the beach is a short walk along the sand to the south.

 Molyvos Delphinia

Delphinia Hotel and Bungalows
www.hoteldelfinia.com
info@hoteldelfinia.com
Tel: 00 30 2 2530 71315 or
00 30 2 2530 71502/3

Kos

Tropical beach

Near Kardamena, on the south coast

A fine sandy bare beach with sunbeds and umbrellas for hire. A taverna sells drinks and light snacks. The **sea is clear** and the swimming is good, although there is a line of **sharp stones** at the water's edge. Either wear sandals or use the simple makeshift access built by the bar owner when you go skinny-dipping.

Take the **coast road south-west** from Kardamena for 3 kms. Pass the Lagas Aegean Village holiday complex and in 600 metres watch for a track on the left signposted 'Tropical Beach'.

The 'A' category **Lagos Aegean Village** is a large hotel well suited to families and has indoor and outdoor pools, tennis courts, gym, and sauna. A complimentary bus service runs round the village. It is 15-20 mins walk from the bare beach.

 Tropical beach

Lagos Aegean Village
www.alphatravel.com
Libra Holidays

Taking the plunge: a tourist in Greece follows the locals for a spot of cliff diving. Although the country does less to promote its bare beach attractions than many of its neighbours, it is one of the most beautiful and peaceful places in the world to get an all-over tan

1 Faliraki nude beach
2 Tsambika
3 Kalathos

Danae Hotel
www.vidado.com
inform@rodos.com
Tel: 00 30 22410 85969 or
00 30 22410 23340
Fax: 00 30 22410 85981
Greece.com, Oasis-hotel.gr

Muses Hotel
www.vidado.com
Tel: 00 30 22410 85303
Fax: 00 30 22410 85625
Kosmar Holidays

Atrium Palace Hotel
www.rodos.com/atrium
www.vidado.com
Libra Holidays, Olympic

The naturist hotel **Vritomartis** in Crete, right, is popular among nude beach lovers who want a bit more of an all-round experience with their bare bathing. Picture courtesy of the hotel: www.naturism-crete.com

Rhodes

Faliraki nude beach

South of the centre of Faliraki

A well known and **easy-to-get-to** bare beach, but a world away from the boisterous excesses of the nearby town. In places there are large outcrops of rock along the shore, but with good **sandy areas** behind for sunbathing. Taverna, toilets, shower, sunbeds and umbrellas are all available. The beach is usually well managed.

Travel south from the town centre and turn left at the traffic lights, then bear left at the fork. At the next junction turn right past Muses Hotel and look for the signpost **Nudist Beach – FKK Strand**.

The 3-star privately owned **Danae Hotel**, set in pretty gardens, is 2 kms from Faliraki. It is the closest accommodation to the nude beach, which is less than 10 mins walk. The 3-star **Muses Hotel** is 1 km outside town and 1.5 kms from the nude beach.

Tsambika beach

Between Kolibia and Arhangelos, on the east coast

A **breathtakingly beautiful** golden sandy beach surrounded by tree-covered cliffs and hills. The shore is sheltered and slopes gently into clear blue sea – perfect for **paddling and swimming**. It gets very busy and bare bathers use the southern corner of the bay – 650 metres from the car park and beach tavernas.

Travel **south from Rhodes town** on the east coast for 25 kms, passing Faliraki en route. The turn for the beach is signposted 2 kms after Kolibia.

Kalathos beach

Near Lindos, on the east coast

A mainly shingle beach stretching for an **almost-deserted** 5 kms to Haraki. There is a **taverna and sunbeds** for rent on the main clothed beach, but by walking north it's easy to find your own personal bare space far from the madding crowd. Swimming is good, but **footwear is advisable** for tender feet.

Travel 3 kms **north from Lindos** to Kalathos and turn right at the sign for Ostria Taverna. At the roundabout turn left down to the beach. Park and walk to the left (north).

The **Atrium Palace Hotel** at Kalathos offers luxury accommodation within an easy walk of the bare area. It has indoor and outdoor pools and a new thalasso spa opening in 2004. Also new in 2004 are the **Atrium Palace Villas**, each with its own private swimming pool and walled garden.

Bare beauties

> **If you want a beautiful setting for a beautiful experience, try skinny-dipping at one of our favourites**

1. Cayo Largo, Cuba
2. Arnaoutchot, France
3. Playa Risco del Paso, Fuerteventura (Spain)
4. Playa Illetas, Formentera (Spain)
5. Les Grottes Plage, France
6. Club Orient beach, St Martin

Best to bare

Cayo Largo, Cuba

Sometimes being naked is not enough. There are things to do, places to see, families to please, whether or not they're wearing anything. If you're looking for some added inspiration, look no further than our top choices for bare beach holidays. More selections on pages 150-151

∨ Turn up, strip off

Gone are the days when you had to trek for half a day to find a secret bare beach. You won't work up a sweat getting to these

1. La Grand Cote, near Royan, France
2. Playa los Tusales, Costa Blanca, Spain
3. Haulover Beach, Florida, USA
4. Vera Playa, Costa de Almeria
5. Sougia, Crete. It's a drive to get here but the town's right on the beach

Sougia, Crete

Mini break, max exposure

Need some colour in all four cheeks? Surprise your partner's socks off with a quick break to a nude beach
1. Ibiza's bare beaches are 2 hours by plane from London
2. Berck sur Mer on France's northern coast
3. La Jenny, near Bordeaux
4. Es Trenc, Mallorca
5. Benalnatura, Costa del Sol

I want to be alone

If you want to get away from everything and everyone, going bare on these uncrowded beaches should fit the bill
1. Rarawa beach, Northland in New Zealand
2. Playa de Castilla South, Matalascanas, Huelva in Spain
3. Cayo Largo, Cuba
4. Lighthouse beaches, Fuerteventura in the Canary Islands
5. St Paul's in Crete

Aguas Blancas, Ibiza

Happy families

Never search for that stray sock again... the nude resorts of Europe are great for families, but there are other places besides
1. Euronat, French Atlantic coast
2. Aphrodite, Leucate Plage, near Perpignan, France
3. Playa Son Bou, St Jaime, Menorca
4. Lighthouse Beach, Long Island, New York
5. Serignan Plage, near Beziers, France

Picture below: Nicole Lejeune, Maison de la France

St Paul's, Crete

Family friendly in France

Croatia

Croatia

Croatia's lovely Adriatic coastline has more than a thousand islands just waiting to be discovered. Crystal clear seas and bare beaches galore have long made it a favourite for discerning holidaymakers. There are literally hundreds of nude and swimsuits-optional places dotted along the coast. Many hotels have their own bare beach, or a public one nearby.

The war and political unrest in the region during the early 1990s sadly had a devastating effect on tourism, though thankfully it is now enjoying a rapid recovery and travellers are returning to their favourite haunts. Surprisingly, we Brits have been more hesitant to take the plunge than some of our continental neighbours, but that's all changing.

And, interestingly, Croatia is tipped as the new hip destination. Not surprising, given the wonderful Venetian influence that can be seen in so many buildings in the towns along the coast – and of course all of these beautiful bare beaches. It's still extremely good value, with more and more holidays and charter flights available from the UK. Go before it loses that special charm.

The Croatian tourist board goes out of its way to help promote the fabulous bare bathing opportunities in the country, producing guides and brochures. All pictures in this section, unless otherwise stated, are supplied by the tourist board: www.croatia.hr

Istria

Kanegra nude beach

Piran Bay, north of Umag

A pebbly bare beach with **lovely clear water** in a natural setting within the Kanegra Holiday Village. The popular resort has 232 bungalows and a campsite, which together provide a range of sports and other activities. There is also a swimsuited beach because the resort is not a nudist centre. A small charge is made for non-residents to use the bare beach and other facilities.

From **Umag** drive 10 kms north on the coast road through **Savudrija** and shortly afterwards **Kanegra Holiday Village** is clearly signposted on the left.

Sol Polynesia nude beach

Katoro, north of Umag

An unusual **stone and grass** bare beach within a mainstream holiday centre. Smooth sunbathing terraces have been constructed on the rocks at the water's edge to enable all-over tan fans to relax in comfort. Trees in the grass areas provide welcome shade. A **cafe** at the bare beach provides refreshments. The nude area is a favourite of Italian and Slovenian visitors, whose borders are only 45 mins and 15 mins drive – summer weekends are **particularly busy**. Small charge for non-residents.

From Umag drive 3 kms north on the main coast road and the Sol Polynesia resort is signposted on the left.

Sol Polynesia Village has 686 bungalows and apartments and is operated by Sol Melia, the giant Spanish hotel company. It is an ordinary clothed resort with a main swimsuited beach. The bare area is on the edge of the village away from the accommodation.

Solaris beach

On the Lanterna peninsula, north of Porec

A 2 km long rocky bare beach backed by **attractive oak woods** which has man-made platforms for sunning. There are also shingle and pebble inlets. It is part of the Solaris nude holiday centre. **Wear sandals** for swimming to protect feet from sea urchins. Refreshments available. There is a small admission charge for non-residents.

1 Kanegra nude beach
2 Sol Polynesia nude beach
3 Solaris beach

Kanegra Holiday Village
www.istra.com/istraturist
kanegra@istraturist.hr
Tel: 00 385 52 73 21 86
Fax: 00 385 52 73 22 12
Book direct

Sol Polynesia Village
www.istra.com/istraturist
sol.polynesia@istraturist.hr
Tel: 00 385 52 71 80 00
Fax: 00 385 52 71 89 99
Airglobe Holidays, Balkan Holidays

Free as a bird: Croatia has long been a champion of bare beach holidays. Unlikely as it may seem, the Duke of Windsor and Mrs Simpson are said to have started the tradition when they asked if they could swim naked at Kandalora beach in 1936. To this day it remains a famous bare beach

Solaris Camping
www.riviera.hr
riviera@riviera.hr
Tel: 00 385 52 408 000
Fax: 00 385 52 451 440
Book direct

Hotel Fortuna
www.riviera.hr
riviera@riviera.hr
Tel: 00 385 52 45 17 22
Fax: 00 385 52 45 11 19
Thomson, Holiday Options, Riviera
Holidays (Croatia)

Zelena Laguna Camping
www.plavalaguna.hr
ac.zelenalaguna@plavalaguna.hr
Book direct

Bijela Uvala Camping
www.plavalaguna.hr
ac.bijelauvala@plavalaguna.hr
Book direct

Hotel Albatros
www.plavalaguna.hr
albatross@plavalaguna.hr
Tel: 00 385 52 41 05 61
Fax: 00 385 52 41 06 02
Balkan Holidays

Hotel Parentium
www.plavalaguna.hr
parentium@plavalaguna.hr
Tel: 00 385 52 41 15 00
Fax: 00 385 52 45 15 36
Balkan Holidays, Holiday Options

Travel north from **Porec** on the main coast road for 12 kms. Clear direction signs to the holiday centre and beach will be seen on the left side of the road.

Solaris Camping is a big nude site with space for 2,000 tents and caravans. Apartments and pavilions are also available to rent, all within a few metres of the bare beach.

Sveti Nicola nude beach

On the islet of the same name, offshore from Porec
A lovely well established bare beach which, like many in Croatia, consists of limestone rocks with flat areas designed for sunbathing. There are places to access the **translucent sea** and the **snorkelling is excellent**. The views are beautiful.

Regular ferry boats sail to the island from **Porec** harbour – the journey only takes five minutes. The beach is on the south side, near to the **Hotel Fortuna**, which is popular with British holidaymakers. The bare beach is almost next to it, a short walk along the coastal path.

Zelena Laguna and Bijela Uvala beaches

Plava Laguna, south of Porec
These two **attractive nude beaches** are close to each other and have ordinary (clothed) campsites next to them. The rocky beaches are terraced and have **shrubs and lush grass** behind them. Paved sunbathing areas have been provided.

Travel south from **Porec** and in 6 kms follow the direction signs to Zelina Laguna.

Zelena Laguna Camping has a good range of facilities and an area of its blue flag beach is reserved for bare beachbums.

Bijela Uvala Camping is eco-friendly and located on an attractive peninsula. A section of its blue flag beach is available for nude relaxation.

The 2-star **Hotel Albatros** at Plava Laguna has 434 rooms and is a short walk from the bare beach.

The 3-star **Hotel Parentium** at Plava Laguna is situated on a tree-covered peninsula 5 kms from the centre of town, but connected by a road-train service. The hotel has a nude terrace for residents and is a 2 km walk along the coast from the bare beach.

Funtana beach

Close to the fishing village of the same name, south of Porec
A super bare beach on a natural peninsula with **crystal clear water** and little **islets nearby** ideal for swimming to. The usual rocky foreshore is backed by **grass and trees** and is part of a

campsite that has a clothed section and a nude section. Small admission charge for non-residents.

The beach and campsite are signposted off the coast road on the right, 7 kms south of Porec.

Funtana Camping is a beautiful and natural site well equipped for tents, caravans and motor homes. You can pitch **right by the water's edge**.

Koversada beaches

Lim Fjord, outskirts of Vrsar

A choice of rock or **imported sand** beaches at this famous nude resort. The first and biggest naturist centre in Croatia, catering for up to 7,000 people, opened in 1961. There's also a small **bare island** reached by footbridge. A wide choice of accommodation, restaurants, bars and shops available. Plenty of space for camping. Volleyball, basketball, table tennis, and lots of water sports are on offer. Admission charge.

Easy to find on the southern outskirts of **Vrsar** – follow the directions from the town centre.

Valalta beach

Lim Fjord, near Rovinj

An attractive bare beach across the water from Koversada. **Valalta** is another famous and long established naturist resort with **lots of facilities** including a super swimming pool close to the shore. A man-made sandy beach provides an alternative to the rocky coastline. Apartments, pavilions and camping have a backdrop of vineyards and cultivated fields. It was awarded overall '**Best Camping in Croatia 2003**' by the National Chamber of Commerce.

1. Sveti Nicola
2. Zelena Laguna & Bijela Uvala
3. Funtana beach
4. Koversada beaches
5. Valalta beach

Funtana Camping
www.istra.com/funtana
camping@riviera.hr
Tel: 00 385 52 44 51 23 (summer)
00 385 52 43 49 00 (winter)
Fax: 00 385 52 44 53 06 (summer)
00 385 52 45 14 40 (winter)
Book direct

Koversada
www.koversada.com
koversada-camp@anita.tdr.hr
Tel: 00 385 52 44 13 78
Fax: 00 385 52 44 17 61
Peng Travel

Valalta
www.valalta.hr
valalta@valalta.hr
Tel: 00 385 52 80 48 00
Fax: 00 385 52 81 14 63
Peng Travel

Croatia's best campsite in 2003 was nudist, which will come as no surprise to anyone who knows the country. **Valalta**, left, has a fabulous pool right by the sea. Picture supplied by the resort

Monsena
www.istra.com/jadranturist
monsena@jadran.tdr.hr
Tel: 00 385 52 80 03 76
Fax: 00 385 52 81 34 97
Peng Travel

Villas Rubin
www.istra.com/jadranturist
fn-villas-rubin@jadran-turist.tel.hr
www.htz.hr
Tel: 00 385 52 80 14 00
Fax: 00 385 52 81 33 53
Book direct

Hotel Sol Club Istria
www.istra.com/jadranturist
hotel-istra@jadran-turist.tel.hr
Tel: 00 385 52 80 25 00
Fax: 00 385 52 81 34 84
Transun-Croatia, Holiday Options,
Airglobe Holidays, Cosmos

Monsena beach

North-west of Rovinj
Another well-known **naturist resort** with its own bare beach. Lots of facilities including a swimming pool with an impressive water slide. There's even a **small harbour** for nudist sailors to tie up their craft. Good quality accommodation. Day visitors welcome.

Villas Rubin bare beach

South-east of Rovinj
A clothed **holiday village** on the coast with 850 bungalows and apartments built in **traditional Istrian style** and operated by Sol Melia, the Spanish hotel group. In addition to a large 'swimsuits' beach there is a pretty area on the edge of the resort reserved for the more discerning bare bathers.

Maschin beach

Red Island, near Rovinj
Maschin is the smaller of two islands connected by a short causeway. The whole nude islet is just waiting for intrepid bare

explorers. It is covered in pinewoods and has a **picturesque shoreline** offering a choice of places for all-over tanning. Visitors love it. During summer the nearby **Hotel Sol Club Istria** runs a snackbar on Maschin.

Ferry boats from **Rovinj** take 15 mins to reach Red Island. Walk round the main island and **across the causeway** to Maschin.

The 4-star **Hotel Sol Club Istria** on Red Island has long been a favourite of British holidaymakers. Quality accommodation in a delightful setting. It also has its own clothed beaches, but is only a short walk from Maschin.

Sveti Katrina bare beach

On the island of the same name, close to Rovinj
A pretty bare area on a series of flat rocks at the edge of the water. This popular beach attracts plenty of nudes so **get there early** because the best spots are limited. Refreshments and toilets nearby.

Use one of the shuttle boats from **Rovinj harbour** – the crossing to Katrina takes

5 mins. Then follow the footpath to the western side of the island, a 15 mins walk.

The luxury 136-room **Hotel Katarina** was completely rebuilt in 2000 and is only a short stroll from the nude beach area.

Rabac bare beach

Outside Rabac village, north-east of Medulin
This lovely long clothes-optional beach where most go bare is at the end of a string of small bays backed by **lush Mediterranean vegetation**. Stretching over 1,500 metres of rocky shoreline interspersed with little pebbly coves, it has glorious scenery and great views across to the **island of Cress**. There are two snack bars just above the beach for refreshments – a swimsuit or light cover-up is required.

The beach is **easily accessible** and has a large car park within 150 metres. Just take the coastal road out of the former fishing village heading east past the Hotel Neptun on the outskirts. The beach is reached shortly afterwards. Look out for the 'FKK' sign.

The recently built **Hotel Neptun** is a 3-star property with 155 rooms. There are lots of sports and other facilities available. It is only 300 metres from the bare beach.

Aparthotel Pluton next to the Hotel Neptun has 176 units many of which have been refurbished for the 2004 season. It's 400 metres from the nude beach.

Kvarner region

Drazica nude beach

Outskirts of Krk town on the island of the same name
A pretty pebble and stone bare beach backed by pinewoods on a quiet stretch of shore just **10 minutes' walk** from the centre of town.

From **Krk** town centre just follow the coast path in the direction of the Hotel Drazica and look out for 'FKK' (German for nudist) signs.

Hotel Drazica has 118 bedrooms and 18 apartments. It is very close to the bare beach.

Suncana Uvala beach

Near Mali Losinj, on the island of Losinj
The name of this nude pebble beach translates as **Sunny Cove**, which is rather apt for bare beachbums. There are many more au

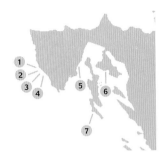

1. **Monsena beach**
2. **Sveti Katrina**
3. **Maschin beach**
4. **Villas Rubin**
5. **Rabac**
6. **Drazica**
7. **Suncana Uvala**

Hotel Katarina
www.hotelinsel-katarina.com
info@hotelinsel-katarina.com
Tel: 00 385 52 80 41 00
Fax: 00 385 52 80 41 11
Inghams, Holiday Options

Hotel Neptun
www.istra.com/rabac
sales@rabac-hotels.com
Tel: 00 385 52 87 22 77
Fax: 00 385 52 87 25 69
Book direct

Aparthotel Pluton
www.istra.com/rabac
sales@rabac-hotels.com
Tel: 00 385 52 86 25 30
Fax: 00 385 52 86 25 36
Book direct

Hotel Drazica
www.hotelikrk.com
Tel: 00 385 51 23 13 24
Fax: 00 385 51 65 57 55
Interhotel.com

1 **Kandalora beach**

2 **Stolac, Sahara and Ciganka**

Hotel Aurora
www.jadranka.hr
hotel.aurora@jadranka.hinet.hr
Tel: 00 385 51 23 13 24
Fax: 00 385 51 23 15 42
Book direct

Hotel Vespera
www.jadranka.hr
hotel.vespera@jadranka.hinet.hr
Tel: 00 385 51 23 13 04
Fax: 00 385 51 23 14 02
Book direct

Suha Punta
www.tzg-rab.hr
Tel: 00 385 51 72 41 33
Book direct

Hotel San Marino Village
www.imperial.hr
sanmarino@imperial.hr
Tel: 00 385 51 77 51 44
Fax: 00 385 51 77 51 28
Book direct

naturel spots nearby: **Zlatna Uvala** (Golden Cove), **Srebrna Uvala** (Silver Cove) and **Cikat** to mention just a few. With a network of well-marked footpaths through the **aromatic maquis** and pine forest it's easy to find your very own deserted buff bay.

On the south coast of the island, 1.5 kms south-west of Mali Losinj, there are two sister hotels, both 3-star, within 200 metres of Suncana Cove – **Hotel Aurora** and **Hotel Vespera**, which are close to the Veli Zal sports centre.

Kandalora beach

Palit, a suburb of Rab town on the island of Rab
This world famous bare beach is where the **Duke of Windsor** and **Mrs Simpson** swam au naturel in August 1936. It is often referred to as the **English Beach** and includes three coves, stretching for 1,500 metres in total. Bar and restaurant available.

The beach is on the southern side of the **Frkanj peninsula**, where a regular ferry from **Jablanac** on the mainland calls, making day visits possible.

The **Suha Punta** holiday village is close to the bare beach and has two sister hotels, **Carolina** and **Eva**.

Stolac, Sahara and Ciganka beaches

Lopar, on the north-western tip of the island of Rab
Sandy beaches are a rare phenomenon in Croatia. However here at Lopar there are no less than 22 of them, including three undeveloped nude ones. The water is shallow, calm and clear making it ideal for **families with young children**. Adults will also enjoy fine skinny dipping.

From the town of **Rab** drive north-west for 13 kms to the tip of the island. The bare beaches are dotted around the Lopar Peninsula. Running from east to west they are **Stolac**, **Sahara** and **Ciganka**.

The **Hotel San Marino Village** at Rajska Playa (Paradise Beach) is close to the bare beaches – Stolac is the nearest, just a stroll away.

Croatia's rocky coastline has easy access to the sea. Picture by keen Polish naturists and Croatian holidaymakers Przemek and Joanna – they are keen to hear from other bare beach users around the world: fansgolasy123@go2.pl

Punta Skala
www.puntaskala.hr
marketing@puntaskala.hr
Tel: 00 385 23 21 12 48
Fax: 00 385 23 21 31 07
Book direct

Crvena Luka
cluka@zdadarnet.hr
Tel: 00 385 23 38 31 06
Fax: 00 385 23 38 49 15
Kompas d.d. (Croatia)

Medena Hotel
www.dalmacija.net/seget/h_medena.htm
Tel: 00 385 21 88 05 88
Fax: 00 385 21 88 00 19
Transun

Hotel Nimfa
www.cursor.hr/pa.nsf/pages/
                    hotnimfa-zivog
hotel-nimfa@st.hinet.hr
Tel: 00 385 21 62 70 55
Fax: 00 385 21 62 71 79
Book direct

North Dalmatia

Punta Skala nude beach

Petrcane, north of Zadar

An attractive rock and gravel **bare beach with showers** at the **Punta Skala** holiday resort. The hotel, bungalows and apartments used to be a dedicated naturist centre until 1989, when it was sold and the new owners changed it into an **ordinary clothed resort**. There is a 'swimsuits' beach as well as the nude one and all of the facilities are in the dressed part of the centre.

Punta Skala is signposted from the village of **Petrcane**, which is 5 kms north of the historic town of Zadar.

Crvena Luka nude beach

Near Biograd, south of Zadar

This pretty beach of **sand and pebbles** is at **Crvena Luka** holiday centre. The bare beach is on the north side of the bay. The hotel, apartments and campsite accommodate 2,000 guests.

From **Zadar** drive 25 kms south down the coast to the village of **Biograd**. Continue through Biograd for a further 5 kms and watch for the signs to **Crvena Luka** resort.

Sveta Katerina

Small island off-shore from Biograd

The islet of **Sveta Katerina** (St Catherine) is completely and utterly bare! There are rocky beaches and lots of trees for shade. Taxi boats run from the quayside in **Biograd**.

Sabunike beach

Sabunike village, north of Zadar

Another rare (in Croatia) **sandy and intimate** beach for nude sunseekers. It is about 10 minutes' walk north from the village centre, while the main 'swimsuits' beach is to the south of town.

Travel north from **Zadar** for 13 kms to the village of **Nin**, then 3 kms west to **Sabunike**.

The town of **Split**, right, is the hub of southern Croatia. It's a great gateway for the bare beaches, but worth visiting in its own right for **Diocletian's palace** and the many churches and bell towers

Central Dalmatia

Medena nude beach

Seget, near Trogir, north of Split

A typical Croatian pebble bare beach which is near the Medena holiday village. This popular strand has lovely views and there are **restaurants** and **watersports** at the nearby clothes-required beach.

A regular bus from **Split**, 30 kms to the south, takes just over half an hour and the Split international airport is only 7 kms away.

The 3-star **Medena Hotel**, which has 680 rooms, is a very short walk from the bare beach.

Nimfa nude beach

Zivogosce, Makarska

This rock and pebble bare beach set in **picturesque scenery** is close to the hotel of the same name.

The 3-star **Hotel Nimfa** is a large property with 560 beds in a main building and adjacent bungalows.

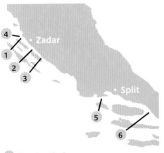

1. Punta Skala
2. Crvena Luka
3. Sveta Katerina
4. Sabunike
5. Medena
6. Nimfa

Dole Camping
auto-camo-dole@st.hinet.hr
Tel: 00 385 21 62 87 49
Fax: 00 385 21 62 87 50
Book direct

Hotel Elaphusa, Hotel Borak
and **Hotel Club Bonaca**
www.zlatni-rat.hr
inf@zlatni-rat.hr
Tel: 00 385 21 63 52 88
Fax: 00 385 21 63 51 50
Holiday Options, Transun, Balkan
Holidays

Apartments Villa Diana
and **Hotel Kactus**
www.supetar.hr or
www.hrvaska.net (agency)
info@supetar.hr or info@hrvaska.net
Tel: 00 385 21 63 11 33 or
00 386 15 12 18 25
Fax: 00 385 21 63 13 44 or
00 386 15 12 18 25
Transun, Hrvaska.net
(Croatian travel agent)

Dole nude beach

Between Zivogosce and Igrane, Makarska
This bare beach is one of the most popular in the region and is located at the western edge of the Dole Campsite.

From **Makarska** travel south on the coastal highway. After 10 kms you'll pass through Igrane. **Dole Camping** is a further 3 kms on the right before **Zivogosce**.

Paklina

Zlatni Rat, Bol on the south coast of the island of Brac
This beach is so **picturesque** that the Croatian tourist board regularly use it in their promotional material. Paklina bare beach is on the western end of **Zlatni Rat**, which is often referred to as the '**golden horn**' because of its dramatic shape. Pine trees provide the backdrop for this lovely spot.

A choice of watersports make it **popular with young people** and it gets very busy in mid-summer. Refreshments are available nearby. There are more **private and secluded coves** for all-over tanning if you continue to walk west beyond Paklina.

Paklina is a short distance west of **Bol town centre**, on the south coast of **Brac**. Small boats ferry passengers from the town to the bare beach or alternatively it is 30 mins walk along the coast.

However, three holiday hotels (run by the same company) are all less than 500 metres from the bare area: **Hotel Elaphusa**, **Hotel Borak** and **Hotel Club Bonaca**.

Supetar bare beach

Supetar, on the north coast of the island of Brac
This is a well used nude beach made up of pebbles and sand. The bare area is adjacent to the **Apartments Villa Diana** and close to **Hotel Kactus**, which are under the same management.

The apartments nearest the bare beach were declared **clothes-optional in 2003** and the company has indicated it may do the same in 2004. The other apartments and the hotel provide ordinary clothed accommodation.

The accommodation and beach are a 15-minute walk from the centre of Supetar.

Jerolim island

Offshore from Hvar
The whole of this rocky islet is a naked paradise – **no clothes required anywhere** apart from the bar. Small ferry boats make regular crossings from the historic town of **Hvar**. It only takes 10 minutes.

There are other bare beaches and islands in the **Pakleni archipelago**, easily reached from town – just look for the boats advertising 'FKK', the German initials for bare bathing. **Stipanska** is another popular choice.

There is no accommodation on the small islands but Hvar town is a beautiful place to stay and handy for the little ferries plying backwards and forwards to the nude beaches and other islands.

The elegant **Hotel Palace** overlooks the harbour and is only steps away from the quayside.

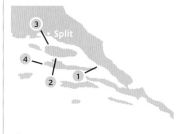

① Dole nude beach
② Paklina
③ Supetar nude beach
④ Jerolim island

Hotel Palace
www.sunnyhvar.com
Tel: 00 385 21 74 19 66
Holiday Options, Transun, Balkan Holidays

Dole (right) is on the **Makarska riviera** (pictures on left), a tourist area with many other bare beaches nestling beneath the stunning mountain of Biokovo

Villas Kolocep
www.holidayoptions.co.uk
info@holidayoptions.co.uk
Tel: 00 385 20 75 70 25
Holiday Options, First Choice

Hotel Sipan
www.sipanhotel.com
info@bosmeretravel.co.uk
Tel: 00 385 20 75 80 00
Saga Holidays, Holiday Options,
Bosmere Travel

Hotel Osmine
www.hotel-osmine.hr
hotel-osmine@du.hinet.hr
Tel: 00 385 20 87 12 44
Holiday Options, Cosmos, First Choice

Hotel Argosy and **Hotel President**
www.babinkuk.com
babinkuk@babinkuk.com
Tel: 00 385 20 44 82 34
Saga Holidays, Holiday Options,
Balkan Holidays

South Dalmatia

Ruza bare beach

Donje Celo, Kolocep, Elafiti islands
A beautiful sandy bare beach on the north-west coast of this car-free island in the vicinity of **Villa Ruza**, which is part of **Villas Kolocep**. One of the most **southerly islands** in Croatia. It is 6 kms from **Dubrovnik** and the ferry calls three times a day.

Sipan bare beaches

Sipan, Elafiti islands
There are many **small and pretty sandy coves** where clothes-optional sunning and swimming have traditionally been the norm on this, the largest of the **Elafiti islands**. Prijezba is a particular favourite.

   Hotel Sipan at **Sipanska Luka** is an ideal base and has its own quay. The nearest sandy beach is 500 metres away, but the secluded bare coves are also nearby. It is 12 kms from **Dubrovnik** and just 1.5 kms from the nearest mainland.

Slano nude beach

Slano, north of Dubrovnik
Set in a beautiful bay by the all-inclusive **Hotel Osmine**, where a section of beach is used for bare relaxation, sunbathing and swimming.

   It's a pleasant walk along the coast from **Slano village**, 41 kms north of Dubrovnik.

Cava beach

Babin Kuk, Dubrovnik
A 300-metre long rock and pebble bare beach with good swimming, situated near the **Hotel Argosy** and **Hotel President**. Although there are no facilities in the nude area, the adjacent **Copocabana clothed beach** has refreshments available.

   It is 6 kms north-west of Dubrovnik town centre on the **Babin Kuk peninsula** and can be reached in about 20 minutes on the number 6 bus from **Pile Gate**, in front of the old town. Get off at the last stop by the Hotel President, take the path past the hotel following the signs to **Copocabana** and on to **Cava**.

Lokrum beach

Lokrum island, offshore from Dubrovnik

An established rocky bare beach with smoothed areas for sunbathing that faces south. It is popular, particularly as the number of nude beaches near Dubrovnik is relatively limited, so it gets busy in summer. There are **quieter spots to be found** by walking a little away from the main nudist area. Occasionally breezy, but otherwise good for swimming – **short ladders** make it easy to get in and out of the sea. Refreshments, showers and toilets nearby. The island has regional park status and is well worth exploring for the **flora and fauna** alone.

Lokrum is reached by ferry from **Dubrovnik old harbour**, regular departures take 10 minutes to make the crossing. On landing turn left and follow the path signposted 'FKK Nude Beach', which is on the **eastern side** of the island. It's 5-10 mins walk.

Mlini nude beach

Betirina, Mlini, south of Dubrovnik

A lovely bare terrace has been built at the water's edge for all-over tanning in this **secluded bay**. It is owned by the nearby

1. Slano
2. Sipan
3. Ruza
4. Cava
5. Lokrum
6. Mlini

There are fewer bare beaches on the mainland near Dubrovnik, but the nearby **islands** more than make up for it

Dubrovnik

1

① **Croatia Hotel**

Hotel Astarea
hoteli-mlini@du.hinet.hr
Tel: 00 385 20 48 40 66
Fax: 00 385 20 48 62 98
Holiday Options, Captivating Croatia,
Balkan Holidays, Saga Holidays

Croatia Hotel
www.hoteli-croatia.hr
info@hoteli-croatia.hr
Tel: 00 385 20 47 55 55
Fax: 00 385 20 47 82 13
Transun, Holiday Options,
Captivating Croatia, Inghams,
Cosmos, Saga Holidays,
Balkan Holidays, First Choice

beach restaurant that takes care of the nude area. It's often said to have a particularly **friendly atmosphere** and welcome shade is available under the pine trees during the hottest part of the day. A real **away-from-it-all feeling** and a wonderful place to recharge your batteries.

Take the airport road south from **Dubrovnik** and in 9 kms arrive at the pretty fishing village of **Mlini**. From the harbour follow the local coast road that goes south past the Hotel Astarea and ends just afterwards. It is then a short walk to the bare area. The nearest parking is at the hotel. Alternatively, use a taxi boat from Mlini harbour – enquire at the **Hogar coffee bar**.

The 3-star **Hotel Astarea** has 217 rooms and is set in woodlands overlooking the sea. It has an indoor pool, sauna, massage, fitness center and lots of sports. Popular with British visitors.

Croatia Hotel nude beach

Cavtat, south of Dubrovnik
An attractive bare beach that has **smoothed areas** built on the rocks for sunbathing. Although out of town it has all the facilities of the hotel to hand. The **swimming is excellent**.

Cavtat is 18 kms south of **Dubrovnik**, not far from the **Montenegro border**. The bare beach is on the western side of the **Sustjepan peninsula**, a 35-minute brisk walk from Cavtat town. An easy option is to drive or take a taxi to the hotel.

The **Croatia Hotel** is a deluxe property with 480 rooms, indoor and outdoor pools and lots of sports and leisure activities on offer.

Only natural

Like throwing off your shoes after a hard day at the office, throwing off your clothes and running naked into a sparkling sea is a certain way to drop that everyday stress.

Today, two of life's greatest luxuries are time and freedom. Bare beaches are the ultimate in both. Time to unwind, refresh the body and relax into a slow and gentle pace of life, in harmony with the rhythmic sound of waves rolling on to the shore. And freedom to stretch out and absorb the warmth of the sun on your entire body, no one telling you what you should and shouldn't wear.

It's the dream way to enjoy the company of your partner, family and friends, or simply let your thoughts and being blend with the surrounding environment.

For a new generation daring to bare is now acceptable, fun and invigorating. As a result, thousands of people are seeking out beaches to experience the first feeling of going bare, swimming without a costume and tanning without marks on their body.

Nude sunbathing is already a mainstream activity across much of the continent and a central part of modern

holidays for many families. The wide access to bare beaches across the world is indicative of our growing wish to live closer to nature and to be happier with ourselves.

Bikinis and one-pieces don't make you look any slimmer – and why should you have to worry about that anyway on holiday? A happily brown woman on the beach looks far better just as she is. And men's tight swimming costumes will never look as fashionable as an all-over tan. No question.

Remote tracts of nude beaches which were once the preserve of the pioneering naturist have evolved into accessible sweeps of unspoilt shores. Holiday resorts know a good thing when they see it. Countless hotels have set aside parts of their beach for discerning nude bathers – in the Caribbean it's now commonplace to find a bare beach among a resort's facilities.

Holistic living and adventure are two of the most sought-after holiday experiences. To walk down a beach with absolutely nothing, your clothes left far behind, is to experience nature in the raw and is an ultimate adventure in itself. But to enjoy the sun, sand and sea without the constraints of clothes allows the body and mind freedom to feel inner peace and calm.

We evolved from the water, and we evolved without clothes. Being bare on the beach is the most beautiful way to return to our natural state.

Portugal

A good place for beach holidays in
Europe is almost always a good place
for bare beaches too. The **Algarve**
has some of the nicest spots for
discerning skinny-dippers. Bottom
picture courtesy Quinta da Horta
holiday centre

Portugal

Nude beaches were unheard of a few decades ago, but now there are many official and popular places for simply being yourself. Even better, many secluded beaches are empty, even on sunny days. This is some of Europe's finest coastline and yet the beaches are often bare in every sense of the word.

The Algarve, on the southern coast, is the jewel in the crown for many holidaymakers. It's full of beautiful beaches, rocky inlets, hills and clifftops, cosmopolitan marinas, trendy cafes, fine restaurants and designer shops. It is also home to some fine golf courses, but there are plenty of hidden bays and fabulous coves that have yet to become major tourist spots.

Portugal's capital, Lisbon, on the west coast, draws culture vultures rather than beach buffs. But even here there are now plenty of places nearby for back-to-nature bathing.

And for creative souls, holidays at a British-owned art school in the Algarve, complete with clothes-optional pool, sunbathing and sauna, are proving a hit. There's no shortage of volunteer models to sit in the sun for the life classes.

More bare beach details are available from www.infolara.com/naturism/beaches.shtml

Meco beach

Alfarim, south of Lisbon

This official bare beach just south of Lisbon is a popular and **well-known destination** for beach lovers, attracting both tourists and locals alike. It's backed by a high cliff and has **springs** that are said to be safe to drink – follow the locals. The white sand is resting place for a good number of bare bottoms on sunny days, and if you fancy a spot of **bodypainting** there's some fun green mud for skin treatment.

The sea along this coast **can be rough** so take care in the water. This beach is probably more fully naturist in atmosphere than Bela Vista a few miles to the north (next listing).

It's an easy drive from **Lisbon**. Take the main A2 highway south, and 12 kms after crossing the city's huge toll bridge turn right for **Sesimbra**, down the N378. After 6 kms take the right turn for **Alfarim**. It's then 12 kms to Alfarim, where signs direct you to the beaches (Praias).

You can leave your car in the parking area for a **small charge** and head to the beach. The bare area is to the left, after the first spring.

Bela Vista

Caparica, south of Lisbon

Even nearer to Lisbon than Meco beach, this huge official bare beach has **3 kms of white sand** and dunes for you to lose yourself in. You can park right by the beach and in season there is a cafe. If you want to get away from other beach visitors, particularly any **non-nudists**, simply keep walking further south.

From **Lisbon** drive south over the A2 toll bridge and turn off for **Caparica**. Head south again along the coast road. There are turnings off here to the right; **Bela Vista** is the last one, after Praiado Rei, about 7 kms from Caparica. Drive to the end of this dirt road and park. The beach on the left is yours to bare. Alternatively there is a little coastal train for tourists that runs from Caparica; stop 19 for Bela Vista beach.

Ursa

Near Sintra

There are two good reasons to go to Ursa – the bare beach and the Cabo da Roca, **Europe's most easterly point**. Some claim Ursa as Portugal's most beautiful beach – it's certainly beautiful enough to attract a good number of bare bathers despite the walk down. Needless to say it's **completely unspoilt** and

1 Meco beach
2 Bela Vista
3 Ursa

Bela Vista beach during an unseasonal heatwave in February. It's nearer Lisbon but Portugal's naturists often go to Meco beach, not far to the south

1 Caneiros

there is plenty to explore along the **sand and rock coastline**.

Just before you get to the cabo (cape in English) there's a track signposted to **Ursa**; some care may be needed on the road. Park at the end and walk down. The path on the left is easiest but allow a good **half hour to climb back up** to your car. The beach is only a few hundred metres to the north of the cape itself.

Algarve

Caneiros

Ferragudo, near Portimão and Lagoa in the Algarve
This small but almost exclusively bare beach is easy to find and has a fabulous view of **craggy offshore rocks**. A delightful and **safe place to swim** or sunbathe on the yellow sands and watch the seagulls flocking to the rocky islets. You can hire a paddle

boat from the neighbouring Ferragudo town beach for around £5 an hour.

To get to the bare cove, simply walk round the rocks to the right (west) of **Ferragudo town beach**. Access can be a little tricky around high tide but the sea here is safe and warm.

If you're keen on **broadening your creative talents** while taking in the Algarve sun, the **Quinta da Horta** is a short distance from the bare beach. It offers arts and crafts in a nudist-friendly holiday cottage development. Much loved by visitors looking for a simple and natural setting, it has its own studio and a range of art and craft courses. The centre is set in an **organic farm**, which provides food for the gourmet meals, and has a small stable complex. **Massage, yoga, health** and **holistic treatment** holidays can also be arranged. There is a tennis court, swimming pool and sauna,

Quinta da Horta
www.naturist-holidays-portugal.com
enquiries@naturist-holidays-portugal.com
Tel: 00 351 282 461 395
Away With Dune

Caneiros beach, below, is one of the many local bare beaches near the Quinta da Horta holiday cottages, which offers arts and crafts under the Algarve sun. The owners can direct you to other local beaches, pictured opposite, for bare bathing. All pictures courtesy Quinta da Horta

1 Island of Tavira
2 Cabanas Velhas

together with a terrace for sunbathing. It's entirely up to you whether or not you wear anything in the facilities and **peaceful gardens**.

Island of Tavira

Tavira, 25 kms east of Faro
This **beautiful half mile** of official bare beach is popular with tourists from across Europe. The island of Tavira lies just across a short stretch of water from Tavira town, and has **fine white sand** and a **warm sea**.

The island is part of the Ria Formosa natural reserve and has a campsite with cafes next to where the ferry arrives.

Take a short ferry ride from **Tavira town's dock** to the island of Tavira. The beaches are on the **seaward** side of the island. The actual bare section is on the western side of the beach (turn right as you face the sea), but **naked bathing** is common outside the officially bare area.

Cabanas Velhas

About 8 kms west of Lagos, Algarve
Another beautiful, **cliff-backed sandy beach** with lots of

space for naked bathing, beach games and generally taking in the peaceful setting. You'll need to bring your own refreshments. The sand is white, the sea warm in season and the cliffs ideal for **careful scrambling**. Beach users, even among individual groups of beach users, tend to be an **easy mix** of clothed and bare bathers.

Drive west from **Lagos** along the main N125 towards **Vila do Bispo**. After about 7 kms take a left turn for **Burgau**, drive 2 kms to the village and go right at the road junction. Drive a short way, looking out for a narrow lane on the left signposted to **Cabanas Velhas**. You can park right by the beach then walk down to the left.

Among the other unofficial bare beaches, there are two more particularly handy for Lagos. **Prainha**, about 12 kms to the east near **Alvor**, has seen nude use on the left hand (east) side, down a long stairway.

Praia Dona Ana, just to the west of Lagos, is well signposted from the town and has bays next to the main beach where nude bathing often takes place.

Hotel Jardim Atlantico
www.castaways.co.uk
Tel: 00 351 291 820 220
Fax: 00 351 291 820 221
Cadogan, Castaways (UK),
Aeoroscope Holidays

Madeira

Although there are no official bare beaches in Madeira, there is one hotel that is attempting to make up the deficit with a terrace for all-over tanning.

Hotel Jardim Atlantico

Prazeres, south-west Madeira
A modern 4-star hotel located 1,500 feet above the coast. There is a health spa and a naked sunbathing terrace. Most UK brochures do not mention the naturist terrace, even though it's clearly there because guests want it.

Caneiros beach, left, is a popular spot for both bare beach lovers and nesting seagulls. Both pictures courtesy Quinta da Horta

Skin full

> **If you want comfort in numbers, thousands of bare bathers gather at some beaches. For the highest concentrations of naked bodies in the world, try our top five**
1. Cap d'Agde, France
2. Vera Playa, Almeria, Spain
3. Koversada, Croatia
4. Euronat, French Atlantic coast
5. Haulover Beach, Florida, USA

Best to bare

Euronat, France

Sometimes being naked is not enough. There are things to do, places to see, families to please, whether or not they're wearing anything. If you're looking for some added inspiration, look no further than our top choices for bare beach holidays

⌄ Most romantic

You can't get closer than being bare. Here are our top spots for that romantic walk along the sands wearing just a smile
1. Petit St Vincent Island, St Vincent and the Grenadines
2. Eleuthera, Bahamas – just you, your loved one and your own beach
3. Hidden Beach, Mexico
4. Maui Little Beach, Hawaii, USA
5. Couples Tower Island, Ocho Rios, Jamaica

Snorkelling and diving 〉

Make friends with the fish – but remember the sun burns just as brightly as you lose yourself in the undersea world
1. Paya Bay bare beach, Honduras
2. Sunset Waters bare beach, Curacao
3. Sveti Nicola, Porec, Croatia
4. Vritomartis, Crete, Greek Islands
5. Villata, Porto Vechio, Corsica

∨ Winter wonderland

Forgotten what the sun looks like? Forgotten what your partner looks like? Fix both with an escape to the sun
1. Haulover Beach, Florida, USA
2. Australia and New Zealand for long haul – any beach will do!
3. Playa Esmeralda, Fuerteventura, Spain
4. Grand Lido Braco, Jamaica
5. Maspalomas, Gran Canaria, Spain

Croatian coast

La Gomera, Canaries

∨ Mix and match

Prefer to strip but your loved one won't bare it? Fear not, most bare beaches have non-nudes. These are among the most mixed
1. Formentera – the huge Playa Mitjorn has space for everyone
2. La Grande Plage, Ile d'Oleron, western France
3. Playa Cabopino, Cala Honda, Costa del Sol, Spain
4. Corralejo, Fuerteventura, Spain
5. Paradise and Super Paradise, Mykonos, Greek islands

Australia & New Zealand

South Pacific

The islands and countries of the South Pacific have long been pictured as the perfect beach destination. Sand as white and fine as talcum powder, seawater that's as warm as it is clean, palm trees swaying beside coral lagoons... and a million uninhabited islets to explore. Could there be a more inviting place to get naked? Well, only if you know where.

Bare beach lovers have plenty of choice for enjoying both Australia and New Zealand. Naked bathing is part of beach life much as it is in European countries. There are some fabulous beaches that just beg you to ditch your costume and enjoy.

The climate and the surroundings are made for natural living. A lot of the people in the South Pacific islands had never worn a stitch of clothing until the missionaries came along in the 19th century. Today many of the islands, such as Fiji and Tonga, are highly prudish about any sort of nudity.

A couple of warnings for bare bathers here. The sun is incredibly fierce so your safe sun routine needs more care than ever. And Australia has sharks and stingers to contend with along some of its coast. Ask for local information, whether you're bare bathing or not.

Australia

There are lots of gorgeous bare beaches in Australia: more than we can list here. There are plenty of websites available but you might need to hunt around to get an overview of the entire country's bare beaches. Among the sites to look at are

freebeach.com.au/
users.tpg.com.au/users/alexvan/places.html
www.aus-nude.org.au/Beaches.htm

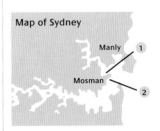

Map of Sydney

① Cobblers beach
② Obelisk beach

New South Wales

Cobblers beach and Obelisk beach

Mosman, Sydney Harbour

Cobblers beach is a small, secluded beach on Sydney harbour where bare bathing is officially welcomed. It's safe for swimming and is **much loved by families** because it has a grassy area for sunbathing, plenty of shaded areas and of course a lovely sandy beach. There is bush behind and walks through Middle Head to enjoy.

Beach life is second nature to most Australians. Bare or not, it's a big part of life and there's plenty of coast for everyone

The beach is near the recently closed **Balmoral naval base** on Middle Head Road in Mosman. Go past the entrance to the base to the oval sports ground with a white picket fence around it. Walk round the **left hand side** of the grounds and you can see the beach. Either take the very steep path down, if you're feeling up to it, or continue along the Middle Head track – it takes less than 10 minutes.

The other beach, **Obelisk**, is also on Middle Head and is larger. It's a white sand beach, popular with bare bathers including many **gay people**, and also has safe swimming. Obelisk beach is to the right of **Middle Head Road**. To get to the beach take the steep path down from the car park

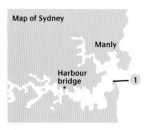

Map of Sydney

Manly

Harbour
bridge — 1

1 Lady Jane Bay

near the end of the road. It's another **pleasant bushland walk**. There are no facilities at either beach so bring provisions.

Lady Jane Bay – or Lady Bay

Sydney Harbour, South Head, Watsons Bay

Lady Jane Bay – also known as Lady Bay – has been a bare beach for more than 40 years. It was one of **Sydney's first nudist beaches**. Despite the name it's also very popular with gay men. The big advantage of this beach – that it's easy to reach – also means that it's **not at all secluded** and is used by many visitors who can't bring themselves to strip off.

There's not much parking at **Watsons Bay**, but you can take buses 324 or 325 from Circular Quay. From Watsons Bay, go to the end of **Old South Head Road**, turn right down Robertson Place and walk to **Camp Cove**. There's a path from here to the beach.

Belongil Beach

North of Byron Bay

Byron Bay is a must for any visitor travelling along the east coast between Sydney and Brisbane. The local council has made sure

www.barebeaches.com

it's also **a must for bare bathers** too, who have been given a lovely bit of coast to themselves. It's a **big sandy beach** with dunes behind and plenty of space for everyone. There's even a little lake just back along the road from the beach, where people also **swim naked**.

It's **easy to find**. To get here, turn off the Pacific Highway about 4-5 kms to the north of the Byron Bay exit, down **Grays Road**. The road goes into the national park and all the way to **Tyagarah Beach** – veer left where the road forks, about three-quarters of the way to the coast. Park at the end and you're there. **Turn right** as you face the sea for bare bathing on Belongil Beach. Tyagarah Beach is on your left. If you're in Byron Bay you can reach the beach by walking north up the coast from the **Byron Bay Beach Club**.

Armonds Beach

Bermagui, south of Narooma, New South Wales south coast
Much cherised by local bare bathers and visitors alike, some say this is the **prettiest nude beach** in Australia. It's set in a curved bay with rocks at either side, lined by **native bush**. If you're travelling between Sydney and Melbourne do stop and bare if you have time. It's officially nude here, and although there are no facilities it's only a 10-minute walk from the car park.

Simply drive south along the coast road from **Bermagui** and **Bermagui South**. About 10 kms along – 3 kms after you've passed **Cuttagee Beach** – take a left down **Kullarro drive** and park at the end. It's an easy track through the bush.

Samurai Beach

Anna Bay, Port Stephens
This is a popular bare beach, partly because it's so beautiful and unspoilt. As with many bare beaches in this country there is an annual **sports day** (this is Australia, remember), which attracts a huge crowd of naked competitors. The beach is over **1 km of golden sand** and is also a good place for surfing and playing other beach sports. But it's not that easy to get to, being up to half an hour's **walk in full sun** from the car park unless you have a four wheel drive. Sky Travel ranks this as one of the 10 best nude beaches in the world, and many visitors – probably those with a suitable vehicle – would agree.

This area is three hours' drive north of Sydney. The bare beach is to the east of **Anna Bay**, near Nelson Bay, **Port Stephens**. Park in Gan Gan Road at Anna Bay; it's the nearest point if you're going to walk.

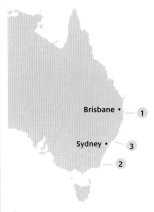

1 Belongil Beach
2 Armonds Beach
3 Samurai Beach

1 Maslin Beach

Alexandria Bay, in Noosa, is tucked away in a beautiful national park

South Australia

Maslin Beach

South of Adelaide

A bit of history was made in 1975 when Maslin became Australia's **first legal nude beach**. It's well known and fairly near the city, so it does attract many bare bathers – and some curious non-nude visitors. The **white sand** is backed by tall cliffs. Families may find access tricky but the safe swimming makes up for the walk, as do occasional visits by **dolphins**. The water is clear and great for snorkelling. There is a van that sells **drinks and ice creams** during summer weekends. Although it can get very busy, it is large enough for everyone to find their bit of bare bathing peace.

The beach is **not the easiest place to find** but a good map will help. Drive south from Adelaide along Main South Road. After about 45 kms turn right into **Maslin Beach Road**, then first left into **Commercial Road**. Follow the signs to the car park at the end and walk down the 100 steps to the beach. If you want easier directions, simply drive to the main (clothed) Maslin beach and walk south (left, facing the sea) to the bare area.

www.barebeaches.com

Western Australia

Swanbourne

Perth, very near the city centre

Hugely popular, partly because it's so near the city centre and partly because it's a lovely place to bare all. Although up to 1,000 happily naked souls gather here at the busiest weekends, there are **2 kms of white sand** backed by grassy dunes so it's never overcrowded. Just about every person on the beach goes bare. You can buy refreshments from the nearby surf club, or from a vendor who sometimes drives along the beach serving **naked customers**.

You can get here after just 20 minutes' drive from the city centre; all you'll need is a city map. Simply drive to the end of **Grant Street** and park near the surf club here. Bare bathing starts a short walk to the north. If you're without a car or bike, the **207 bus** goes from the city post office right to the surf club.

1 Swanbourne, Perth

Queensland

It's not just the **dangerous jellyfish** that worry bare bathers in this Australian state. Weirdly, Queensland **lacks any official bare beaches**, despite its beautiful, uncrowded coastline and climate. But there are plenty of remote spots for freelance skinny-dipping, and many beaches where bare bathing has been going on for years **without problems**.

Alexandria Bay

Noosa national park, Sunshine Coast

This lovely, **long sandy bay** is in a pretty spot and highly popular with bare beach lovers for year-round sunshine. It's well over a mile from any roads and has been used naked for years. Bare bathers tend to gather at the southern end (right as you face the sea).

You can approach the beach from two directions. If you're coming from **Noosa Heads**, you can start from the national park headquarters' car park and take the 3 kms scenic walk through the bush. If approaching from **Sunshine Beach** to the south, simply walk to the north (left as you face the sea) and take the **track over the headland** at the end. It's another nice walk, and Alexandria Bay is just on the other side.

1 Alexandria Bay
2 North Trinity Beach

North Trinity Beach

Trinity Beach town, north of Cairns

This place is often used unofficially by bathers who'd rather go

Amaroo Beach Resort
www.amarooresort.com
info@amarooresort.com
Tel: 00 617 4055 6066
Fax: 00 617 4057 7992
Interhotel.com

without. The beach is north of Trinity Beach itself, a resort town near **Cairns**. The resort is a handy enough base if you're in the area to explore the **Great Barrier Reef**. Best of all, there is a convenient development nearby that welcomes bare beach goers. The resort can give guests full information on the beach.

Amaroo Beach Resort is a 4-storey apartment development overlooking North Trinity nude beach. Each apartment has a **private area** suitable for au naturel sunbathing. The resort has its own direct access to the beach and is described as naturist-friendly, but it is not a nudist resort. Non-nude facilities include a salt water swimming pool, spa, BBQ and a full-size tennis court.

Victoria

Victoria does have an official beach for baring all called **Sunnyside North**, at Port Phillip Bay, although it's not as popular or easy to find as many of Australia's other bare beaches. There are a couple of handy places to stay in the state too if you want a bit of naked time in the sun.

Jarawong Country Cottages
Yandoit, Central Victoria

A group of five privately owned rural cottages situated in the bush, two hours from Melbourne and close to the Spa Centre of Australia. The property welcomes visitors to sunbathe and swim au naturel, with a designated area set aside for clothes-optional leisure.

Jarawong Country Cottages
www.axs.com.au/~jajarcc/
jajarcc@netcon.net.au
Tel: 00 613 5476 4362
Book direct

Lea Lodge
Montrose, Victoria

This 4-star luxury bed and breakfast establishment offers naturist-friendly accommodation. There is a swimming pool and sunbathing terrace for clothes-optional relaxation.

Lea Lodge
www.users.bigpond.com/lealodge/
lealodge@bigpond.com
Tel: 00 613 9761 9183
Book direct

New Zealand

New Zealand is just about the only place in the South Pacific with **no specific law against being bare** on the beach. As long as you're not disturbing other people, and there aren't any specific prohibitions against nudity, you can strip off and enjoy the country's remote beaches in the most natural way imaginable.

The country's tourist authority recently ran an ad campaign showing a pair of young skinny-dippers dashing into the sea on an empty beach. It sums the country up well.

In fact, New Zealand's **huge and largely empty coastline** has so many bare bathing possibilities it's hard to provide any sort of guide as to where other bare bathers gather. People go bare on virtually all the remote beaches. If you're alone or keep a respectful distance from others and remember to **put your knickers on** before asking someone for the time, you should have no problem finding a place to experience 100% pure New Zealand.

For more beach information, see these websites:
www.top.net.nz/~fbgnz/index.html
homepages.ihug.co.nz/~koenig/nz_nudism/nz_nudism.htm
www.naturist.co.nz/holidays.htm

The Coromandel peninsula, just below Auckland is beautiful and has some fabulously empty beaches ideal for baring all. **Picture**: Joe Gardiner

1 Rarawa Beach
2 Pohutukawa Bay
3 Little Palm Beach
4 Orpheus Bay
5 Opoutere

Little Palm Beach, below, is a friendly place to go bare. Palm Beach, in the distance beyond the rocks, has shops and the bus stop

North Island

Rarawa Beach

Northland, east coast
If you want some solitude and a bare beach in the most literal sense of the world, this **blindingly white sand** beach is well worth the drive. It's so remote you're unlikely to surprise anyone else who makes it here by bathing in the nude. There's certainly **plenty of space** to find somewhere by yourself. And given that the sand is the colour of Tippex just about anyone looks like they've got a nice tan.

From **Kaitaia** drive north for 57 kms until you see the sign to the right for **Rarawa Beach Access**. It's about 4 kms from here to the sea.

The nearest shops and petrol are at **Houhora**, 14 kms back towards Kaitaia. There is a **camping ground** at Rarawa.

Pohutukawa Bay

Auckland north shore
At the north end of **Long Bay beach**, this pretty beach has sand and good shade from the Pohutukawa trees which give the bay its name. It's got **good swimming** and is remote enough for undisturbed bare bathing. If the tide is right in, simply take the path round the cliffs that separate it from the end of Long Bay.

Long Bay is the last of **Auckland's north shore bays**, just past Torbay. There is good access and the bay is easy to find from Torbay: simply follow the **main shopping road** north. At Long Bay regional park, drive to the far end and park – as far north as you can go in other words. It's a 20-30 minute walk north (left as you face the sea).

Little Palm Beach

Waiheke Island
Waiheke is often called Auckland's **island suburb**, and is just 35 minutes by ferry from the city centre. It's well worth a visit for the beautiful countryside and vineyards – and of course to spend some time with the **friendly bare bathers** at Palm Beach. It's well used by locals, who are as welcoming as only Kiwis can be, clothed or not. The swimming is great: the beach is golden sand tucked beside a **rocky headland for snorkelling** and

exploring. In fact it's one of the few beaches in New Zealand where you're **virtually guaranteed** to find other bare bathers on a sunny day.

Catch the **Waiheke ferry** from **Quay Street** in central Auckland. Buses meet the ferries: take the one for Palm Beach if you haven't got your own transport. At Palm Beach, simply walk past the rocks to your left, or over the low headland if the tide is in, and this popular bare beach is all yours. Ferry information from www.fullers.co.nz

Don't forget to **make a note** of the return bus times before you walk to the beach. The buses are all timed to meet ferries, which apparently wait if a bus is late. That's New Zealand for you.

Orpheus Bay

Auckland, west coast to the north of the city

The dark yellow/brown sand and overhanging trees give Orpheus bay an interesting, **secluded atmosphere**. The beach is backed by a steep hill **overflowing with native bush**. You can buy supplies in Huia itself; as with all New Zealand bare beaches the seclusion means you need to bring your own supplies.

From the west Auckland suburb of **Titirangi**, simply follow the signs to Huia, which is 14 kms away along the coast. As the road bends to the right and goes downhill into Huia town there is a sign to the left for **Huia Point Lookout**. Drive down this track and park on the grass. There is a well-trodden path on the left hand side of the parking area. It's slightly hard to spot the entrance to the path, but it's about 150m from the main road, well before you reach the lookout point itself. It won't take you long to find it.

Opoutere, at the start of the Bay of Plenty, is a lovely long beach which just invites you to strip off and enjoy. But when in New Zealand don't forget that the sun can really burn

Opoutere

Western Bay of Plenty

This long sandy beach can seem **virtually empty**, even on sunny summer days. But it's well known to New Zealand's nudists for the fabulous bare bathing, and to other visitors for its nature reserve and peaceful location.

It's a huge beach. Simply walk to the north (left as you face the sea) and keep going until you're either away from the clad beach users or among other bare bathers, although people go skinny dipping pretty much anywhere along here at times. You might be the only bare bather, or you might

Katikati naturist park
www.katikati-naturist-park.co.nz
sampsons@ihug.co.nz
Tel: 00 64 7 549 2158
Freephone in NZ: 0800 4567 567

be one of several, but **no-one seems to care**, or even notice for that matter.

Opoutere is off a side road from **State Highway 25**, south of **Pauanui** and north of **Whangamata**. Simply drive past the houses that make up Opoutere and follow the road to the parking area at the end; there's a sharp right at the very last bit where the road forks. There is a **wooden footbridge** that takes you into a pine forest. Sandy paths lead to the beach, about 10 mins walk.

There is a campsite and hostel at Opoutere, but buy supplies at Whangamata or elsewhere before you get here.

A beautiful naturist haven worth considering if you're in the Bay of Plenty area is the **Katikati naturist park**. Its owners have created a unique holiday destination with camping and caravans for hire.

There is a pool, sauna and spa and a pretty stream among the native plants. It's a **heavenly place to strip off**, and as long as you're happy to join in a bona fide naturist environment you can just turn up and book in. However, advance booking might be a good idea at busier times of the year.

Orpheus bay, below, is handy for Auckland. The beach is named after a navy ship that was wrecked offshore

www.barebeaches.com

South Island

Mapua Leisure Park

Waimea Estuary, Tasman Bay coast, Nelson

The beach here is attached to a **unique holiday park** where it's entirely up to you whether or not you wear clothes. Some holiday-makers stay dressed, and of course many choose to strip off, particularly on the beach. The park is set in 25 acres of **native woodland** with a range of accommodation including motel rooms, cabins and chalets. The owners say 'the choice and freedom to be clothed or nude lends to the atmosphere which the park has become famous for.' The park has a **swimming pool**, **tennis courts**, cafe, sauna, spa, **nine-hole golf course** and much more.

From **Nelson** take **State Highway 60** to **Mapua**. Turn right into the town, down **Aranui Road**, then take a left down **Toru Street** over the causeway to the leisure park.

Woodend beach

North of Christchurch

One of many long sandy beaches that bare bathers often use in the South Island, listed here mainly because it's so handy for **Christchurch**. You may be the only bare bather on the beach, but it's a huge expanse of coast and if you walk north there's plenty of space to **sunbathe undisturbed**. There are sand dunes and pines behind the beach.

Heading north from Christchurch on **State Highway 1**, turn off for **Woodend** after 24 kms. It's another 3 kms to the town, where there is a shop. Park near the sands and walk to the north (left as you face the sea).

1 Mapua Leisure Park
2 Woodend beach

Mapua Leisure Park
www.nelsonholiday.co.nz
inquiries@nelsonholiday.co.nz
Tel: 00 64 3 540 2666
Fax: 00 64 3 540 3888
Book direct

Woodend beach, near Christchurch, is a peaceful stretch of coast which bare bathers often use

Caribbean & Bahamas

There are plenty of islands in the
Caribbean to satisfy your dreams of
unwinding naked in a peaceful
paradise setting

Caribbean & Bahamas

Renowned for their gorgeous tropical shores and glamorous celebrity lifestyle, the Caribbean and the Bahamas have a host of bare beaches. Combined with so many different cultures, the only problem for all-over tan fans is deciding where to choose. Hotels and holiday resorts know their market and many have now opened clothes-optional beaches inside their private grounds.

Jamaica in particular has all manner of destinations that include somewhere to swim, chill out and relax naked, all within the security of a resort. The island of St Martin is home to one of the most famous bare beaches in the world, while Dutch dependency Bonaire is a favourite of divers, birdwatchers and nudists alike.

The nude look on the beach just gets more and more fashionable, no matter what type of traveller – budget conscious or well-heeled. Tropical islands included.

Note: we haven't included location maps because bare beaches in these islands are usually beside the resorts.

Jamaica

Grand Lido Negril (SuperClubs)

Bloody Bay, Negril on the west coast of the island
A delightfully **secluded white sand cove** at this upscale all-inclusive resort, which is reserved specially for bare bathers. Another beach is available for those who prefer to wear a costume. And it's the same for the two pools – one with swimsuits and one without! Operated by **SuperClubs**, and a recent winner of the Condé Nast readers' choice 'Best Resort' award.

Hedonism II (SuperClubs)

Bloody Bay, Negril on the west coast
Two lovely tropical beaches at this SuperClubs all-inclusive resort, one labelled for nudes and the other for prudes. There is also a spa pool for bare bathers. You can even take a **nude cruise** on the company's own yacht. This resort and its sister, Hedonism III, have a reputation for a particularly **adult orientation** and are popular with swinging couples. However, it's not that over the top, especially in public, and many other holidaymakers simply enjoy the lively party atmosphere.

Hedonism III (SuperClubs)

Runaway Bay, north coast, 35 miles east of Montego Bay airport
A good size nude beach with gleaming white sand and **turquoise sea** is just waiting for buff bathers at this new SuperClubs all-inclusive adult resort. There is another beach for those that prefer to wear a costume.

Grand Lido Braco (SuperClubs)

Trelawny Bay, Rio Bueno, 42 miles east of Montego Bay on the north coast
Not just a beautiful bare beach, but nearly **half the resort** has been designed for relaxation in the buff. Accommodation, a swimming pool, two spa pools, a bar and a clubhouse diner open 24 hours a day are all available on the bare side. In fact, the

All SuperClubs resorts
www.super-clubs.com
info@800gosuper.com
Tel: 020 8290 3600 (UK)
00 1 800 330 8272 (US)
Fax: 020 8313 3547 (UK)
British Airways, Thomson, Kuoni, Hayes & Jarvis, Funway (plus Peng and Canarian Dreams for Lido Braco and Hedonism)

Leave only footprints: bare beaches are said to be cleaner than ordinary beaches because their users take rubbish home with them.
Picture: Joe Gardiner

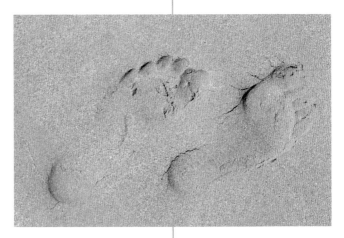

All SuperClubs resorts
www.super-clubs.com
info@800gosuper.com
Tel: 020 8290 3600 (UK)
00 1 800 330 8272 (US)
Fax: 020 8313 3547 (UK)
British Airways, Thomson, Kuoni,
Hayes & Jarvis, Funway (plus Peng
and Canarian Dreams for Lido Braco
and Hedonism)

Sans Souci Resort and Spa
www.sanssoucijamaica.com
reservations@sanssoucijamaica.com
Tel: 001 876 994 1206 / 1353
Fax: 001 876 994 1408
Book direct

Couples Tower Island
www.couplesochorios.com
Tel: 00 1 888 403 2822
Airtours, Thomson, Kuoni, JMC,
First Choice, Virgin

Couples
www.couplesnegril.com
Tel: 00 1 876 957 5960
British Airways, Thomson,
Airtours, Kuoni, JMC

Sunset Beach Resort and Spa
www.sunsetbeachjamaica.com
Tel: 00 1 800 330 8272
Airtours, Thomson, Virgin, Trailfinders

enormous nude pool is the **biggest for skinny-dipping** in the Caribbean. The whole resort is styled like a **traditional Jamaican village** and operated by SuperClubs.

Breezes Golf and Beach Resort (SuperClubs)
Runaway Bay, on the north coast of the island
Two beautiful soft sand beaches, gleaming white in the sun – one of them just for being gloriously bare. What's more, the owners of this SuperClubs resort have thoughtfully built a **romantic nude spa pool** right by the bare beach.

Sans Souci Resort and Spa
Ochio Rios, on the north coast
A lovely clothes-optional beach where swimsuited and bare bathers can relax on the tropical white sand. It is within an all-inclusive resort, which has been **completely refurbished** by the new owners for 2004.

Couples Tower Island
Ocho Rios, on the north coast
A well-known bare island, which features in the Travel Channel's list of **top nude beaches worldwide**. Here at 'Bare Beaches' there's too much competition to award that accolade, but nonetheless it's a wonderful spot. There is a nude pool with a swim-up bar, **double hammocks for romantics** and plenty of loungers for relaxing. The island is privately owned by the hotel and is 200 yards offshore – it has plenty of seclusion for that all-over tan. The courtesy launch will ferry you on request.

Couples
Negril, west coast
On one side of this **lovely destination** is a super tropical bare beach for relaxing and swimming in aquamarine sea. The all-inclusive luxury resort is relatively new, but has already won a **major award** for the quality of its facilities and service, among them of course the choice to sunbathe and swim naked from the beach.

Sunset Beach Resort and Spa
Montego Bay, north-west coast
A private bare cove is one of three beaches at this big holiday centre; the other two are for swimsuit wearers. A **good value** all-inclusive 420-room high-rise resort – recently refurbished. Rooms at the **Beach Inn** are closest to the nude area.

Decameron Club Caribbean

Runaway Bay, on the north coast
A clothing-optional area has been set aside on the **pretty white sand beach** at this popular all-inclusive holiday resort.

Starfish Trelawny Resort

Near Montego Bay
There is a swimsuits-optional beach at this moderately priced all-inclusive family-style resort (owned by SuperClubs). However, it should be noted that the bare beach is reserved for **adults only**.

Point Village Resort

Bloody Bay, Negril
There is a secluded nude cove for buff visitors at this all-inclusive condominium complex (room only accommodation also available). Located between Hedonism II and SuperClub's Grand Lido, but under separate management.

Decameron Club Caribbean
www.decameron.com
lazybutlively@clubcaribbean.com
mercadeo.corp@decameron.com
Tel: 00 1 876 973 4802
Airtours, Kuoni, Hayes & Jarvis, JMC, First Choice, Virgin

Starfish Trelawny Resort
www.starfishresorts.com
trelawnybeach@bigfoot.com
Tel: 00 1 876 954 2450 or
00 1 800 659 5436
Fax: 00 1 954 925 0334
Kuoni, Virgin, Hayes & Jarvis, Airtours, Thomson, JMC

Point Village Resort
www.pointvillage.com
info@pointvillage.com
Tel: 00 1 876 957 5170
Fax: 00 1 876 957 5351 / 5113
Airtours, First Choice

Carib Beach Apartments
www.jamaicalink.com/carib/
info@caribbeach.com
Tel: 00 1 876 957 4358
Fax: 00 1 876 957 3447
Caribbean Dreams, www.hotels.nl

Firefly Cottages
www.jamaicalink.com
firefly@jamaicalink.com
Tel: 00 1 876 957 4358
Fax: 00 1 876 957 3447
Caribbean Dreams

Secret Cabins
www.jamaicalink.com/secrets
secrets@jamaicalink.com
Tel: 00 1 876 957 9325 or
001 876 957 4358 (out of hours)
Fax: 00 1 876 957 3447
Book direct with owner Audrey Stokes
or through Firefly

Drumville Cove
www.negril.com/dcmain.htm
drumvillecove@hotmail.com
Tel: 00 1 876 957 4369
Fax: 00 1 876 957 0198
Caribbeanmagic.com

Home Sweet Home
www.homesweethomeresort.net
rooms@homesweethomeresort.com
Tel: 00 1 876 957 4478
Hotelsaroundtheworld.com

Catcha Falling Star Resort
www.onestopva.com/catcha/
                    catchamain.htm
Caribbeanmagic.com

Resort Euphoria Sea
www.resorteuphoria.com
info@resorteuphoria-negril.com
Tel: 00 1 440 285 8684
Book direct

Carib Beach Apartments

Rutland Point, Negril
A sandy cove is available for nude sunbathing at this small group of apartments, next to Point Village Resort. The apartments are set in **pretty subtropical gardens** on the beachfront.

Firefly Cottages

Negril
A lovely clothes-optional beach that, unusually on Jamaica, is **open to the public**. Directly in front of the family-run holiday cottage resort, which has **20 air-conditioned rooms**.

To quote from the website: 'Whether you call it au naturel, skinny dipping, topfree, nude or naturist, you can enjoy it here quietly on the beach, in the Jacuzzi or verandah, but best of all in the Caribbean sea. We don't make a big thing out of being privileged to offer you a clothes optional beach...'

On the same bare beach, next door to Firefly, **Secret Cabins** offers bargain low price rooms for the budget traveller. Access to some of the Firefly facilities available.

Drumville Cove

Negril
No bare beach here, but there is a secluded nude **lounging area** on the cliffs above the sea, at this cosy all-inclusive resort.

Home Sweet Home

Negril
Clothes-optional sunbathing is available on **terraces on the cliffs** where chairs and sunbeds are provided. A serviced seaside resort where all 14 rooms have private verandas overlooking the Caribbean. Two accommodation units have **large private balconies** for nude sunning, which are available on request.

Catcha Falling Star Resort

Negril
A private cove for bare bathing is available at this 3-star laid-back resort that has six tropical villas.

Resort Euphoria Sea

Negril
An interesting concept at this new American-owned upscale resort – one week every month is designated a '**nude week**'. The remainder of the time it is an ordinary clothed destination. There are 30 rooms, **all with sea view** and the whole property is au

naturel during nude weeks (dates on the website). A member of the American Association for Nude Recreation. A sister resort, **Euphoria Land**, which is not on the coast, is bare all the time.

Sonrise Beach Retreat

Robins Bay, St Mary, on the north coast
This beautiful undeveloped sandy cove is used for discreet nude bathing, and has its own **deluxe cottage** which sleeps up to five. It is part of an 18-acre **tropical eco-resort** with four other cottages on a remote stretch of coast. Formerly known as 'Strawberry Fields', a counterculture centre in the 1970s, where **Mick Jagger** was reputed to hide out. There is a second, clothed beach.

Bonaire

Sorobon Beach

South-east coast
A delightful shallow bay protected by a barrier reef, ideal for swimming, snorkelling, sailing and windsurfing. The dazzling white sands are part of the **Sorobon Beach naturist resort**, a relaxed haven on this tiny Caribbean island. Sun shelters built from palm trees and gentle trade winds ensure there is always a cool spot in the heat of the day. Parakeets and flamingos abound.

The resort is 5 miles south-east of the capital **Kralendijk**.

Grenada

La Source

St Georges
A **very unofficial** secluded bare beach between the cliffs, a few minutes' walk over the hill from the hotel **La Source** – ask at the hotel before you go. The luxury all-inclusive resort offers a huge range of **health, beauty and spa treatments**.

British Virgin Islands

Havers Villa

South coast of Tortola
Not a beach but somewhere special to relax au naturel or to arrange some **clothes-optional sailing**. A large private family villa which guests share with the owners. It is located 500 feet above the sea. There is a **swimming pool** and clothes and costumes are optional at all times. The owners, Barry and Roz Rice, operate a yacht charter business and can offer bare cruising.

Sonrise Beach Retreat
www.in-site.com/sonrise/
sonrise@cwjamaica.com
Tel: 00 1 876 999 7169 or
00 1 876 776 7676
Fax: 00 1 876 999 7169
Book direct

Sorobon Beach
www.sorobonbeachresort.com
info@sorobonbeachresort.com
Tel: 00 599 717 8080
Fax: 00 599 717 6080
Peng Travel

La Source
www.lasourcegrenada.com
lasource@caribsurf.com
Tel: 0870 220 2341 (UK)
Fax: 020 8878 9124 (UK)
Kuoni, Virgin Caribbean,
Hayes & Jarvis

Havers Villa
www.endlesssummer.com
barry@endlesssummer.com
Tel: 00 1 284 494 3656
Fax: 00 1 284 494 4731
Away With Dune

Meritage Cottage
www.a1vacations.com/
meritagestjohn/3/
Email: via website
Tel: 00 1 340 693 8291
daytime/evening 9am-9pm local time
A1 Vacations (USVI)

Pallina Villa
www.villawebsite.com/v1/pallina.html
Email: via website
Tel: 001 954 783 6605
Fax: 001 801 409 5622
Global Villa Index (USA)

Holiday homes on the US Virgin Islands

There are also three luxury holiday homes with privacy for all-over tanning. Romantic **Meritage Cottage** at Cruz Bay, **St John** is for two people. Overlooking **Hart Bay**, it is 5 minutes' walk from the clothed beach, but the terrace at the cottage has a spa pool and is perfect for nude sunbathing.

Pallina Villa at Magen's Bay, **St Thomas**, is a large recently renovated 4-bedroomed air-conditioned property by the sea. The sweeping terrace is not overlooked and ideal for bare relaxation and sunbathing. The villa has its own swimming pool.

The **Hummingbirds Home** at Tabor and Harmony, **St Thomas** has a self-contained apartment for two in a Mediterranean-style villa, 300 feet above and overlooking the ocean. The apartment opens on to a sundeck and **swimming pool for nude bathing** and sunning. The accommodation is promoted as clothes-optional. It's near Tutu Bay and Sunsi Bay on the north of the island.

Antigua

Hawksbill Hotel bare beach

Hawksbill Bay

A gorgeous hidden bare beach with that wonderful 'away from it all' feeling for au naturel sunbathing. The hotel has no less than four beaches and the bare one is a **short walk** from the accommodation. Be careful of underwater rocks near the shore.

Aruba

Renaissance Aruba island beach

Seaport Village, Orangestad

A **40-acre private island** which has two beaches and

174   www.barebeaches.com

belongs to the hotel. The bare area is at the west end and the journey from the mainland takes 5 minutes in the **courtesy launch**. The modern Dutch hotel is close to the town centre.

St Vincent and the Grenadines
Petit St Vincent Island
40 miles south of St Vincent
A beautiful '**Robinson Crusoe**' island, two-thirds of which is beach. The owners say about nude sunbathing: 'While we are not a clothing-optional resort, the privacy on the patio of the cottages would allow this, and the staff can provide directions to **suitable areas of beach**'. This is an exclusive private estate with 22 luxury cottages on the tiny 113-acre tropical islet.

In 2003 the Sunday Times rated cottage number 18 amongst the **top 10 most romantic** hotel rooms worldwide – so now you know which one to ask for!

Hope Bay, Bequia
Central south coast of Bequia island, 9 miles south of St Vincent
The **archetypal deserted tropical beach** – palm trees swaying in the breeze and white sand gleaming in the Caribbean sun. The beach is a little off the beaten track and requires a **pleasant walk** along the coastal path to get there. You will probably have the bay to yourself and can then enjoy the freedom of relaxing au naturel.

The nearest place to stay is the **Old Fort**, a laid-back hilltop country inn which was formerly a plantation house dating back to the **early 1700s**. It has six en-suite rooms, a swimming pool and fabulous views all set in 30 acres of lush gardens. It is 25-30 minutes' walk from Hope Bay.

Nevis
Oualie Bay
North-west coast of the island
Next to the shore right on the edge of Oualie Bay is the privileged location of **Headlands Cottage**, a lovely two-bedroomed holiday cottage owned by British naturists. They advise that with a little discretion it's fine to go bare in part of the bay. However, it's also practical to enjoy most of the **private grounds** in the buff.

The swimming pool is by the owner's house next-door and suitably screened for skinny-dipping. There's a restored **300-year-old fort** within the grounds. Initial rental enquiries can be sent to the owner of Headlands Cottage by email.

Hummingbirds Home
www.hummingbirdshome.com
hummingbirdhome@vipowernet.net
Tel: 00 1 340 714 39 27
Fax: 00 1 340 714 39 27
Book direct

Hawksbill Hotel
www.hawksbill.com
hawksbill@candw.ag
Tel: 00 1 268 462 0301
Fax: 00 1 268 462 1515
Kuoni Worldwide, Virgin
Caribbean Calypso

Renaissance Aruba
www.renaissancehotels.com
sonesta.europe@wxs.nl or
sonesta4u@aol.com (US)
Tel: 00 2978 36000
Fax: 00 2978 25317
Castaways Travel (USA),
Hoteldiscount.com

Petit St Vincent Island
www.psvresort.com
psv@fuse.net
Tel: 00 1 513 242 1333
Fax: 00 1 513 242 6951
Caribtours, Elegant Resorts,
Caribbean Expressions

Old Fort
www.oldfortbequia.com
info@theoldfort.com
Tel: 00 1 784 458 3440
Fax: 00 1 784 458 3440
Book direct

Headlands Cottage
holland@care4free.net and
holland@caribsurf.com

Sunset Waters
www.sunsetwaters.com
info@sunsetwaters.com
Tel: 00 5999 8641 233
Fax: 00 5999 8641 237
Castaways Travel (USA)

Curacao

Sunset Waters bare beach

North-west coast of the island, 25 miles from the airport
A private area of the beach at this all-inclusive resort is reserved for au naturel bathing. **Sparkling clear sea** makes swimming, snorkelling and diving particularly popular. The whole resort goes entirely clothes optional from time to time, with 2004's 12 days of bare bathing heaven starting on September 14.

St Martin

Orient Bay

North-east coast of the island
This **breathtaking mile-long sweep of white sand** lapped by an aquamarine and turquoise sea is famed for its nudist credentials. Club Orient naturist resort is right on the beach at the southern end of the bay and has been accommodating sunseeking hedonists for over 20 years – and it's now more popular than ever.

As other developments have sprung up in this lovely area, only the **generous section** of sand in front of the resort is bare throughout the day. However, first thing in the morning, residents and earlybirds often start the day by enjoying a naked stroll from one end of the bay to the other.

Lots of watersports, bars and restaurants are available all along the beach. It gets very busy when guests from cruise ships calling at St Martin make a beeline for Orient Bay. If it gets a bit hectic, take a picnic and discover the tranquillity of a nearby uninhabited island by sailing naked – and **thoroughly escape from the 21st century**.

Club Orient claims to be the premiere clothing optional resort in the western hemisphere – well it would wouldn't it – but there is no denying it is a **fantastic location** and offers comfortable self-catering suites, chalets and studios. A shop, bar and restaurant complete the picture.

There are a number of other places to stay in the Orient Bay area. The intimate **3-star Hotel L'Hoste** is on the beach not far from the bare area. The hotel is not naturist but has a relaxed approach to clothes-optional dress in the grounds and by the pool.

Green Cay Village has 16 luxury villas overlooking the beach. It is 5 minutes' drive to the nude section, but several of the villas with pools have sufficient privacy for bare sunning and swimming.

Club Orient
www.cluborient.com
clubo@cluborient.com
Tel: 00 1 590 87 33 85
Fax: 00 1 590 87 33 76

Hotel L'Hoste
www.hostehotel.com
contact@hostehotel.com
Tel: 00 590 87 42 08
Fax: 00 590 87 39 96
Hotelbook.com

Green Cay Village
www.greencay.com
info@greencay.com
Tel: 00 590 29 48 72
Fax: 00 590 87 39 27
Au Naturel Travel (USA), Hotels.nl

Hotel La Plantation has 17 villas set in five acres of tropical gardens on Orient Bay. Its Coco restaurant on the beach has lounge chairs for clothes-optional sunbathing and the main bare beach is 1 km further along. **Cap Caraibes Hotel** has 35 new self-catering suites built by the sea. The nude area at Club Orient is 10 minutes' walk from the apartments.

A very short drive south of Orient Bay, **Caribbean Nature** by Oyster Pond Lagoon and Marina is an informal naturist property. Accommodation is in **garden bungalows** around a swimming pool. French owned and operated. Fine views over the bay and marina. The nearest clothed beach and shops are 150 metres.

Puerto Rico

Palomino Island, Wyndham El Conquistador

Fajardo, Las Croabas
This private offshore island is owned by the **Wyndham El Conquistador Country Club** and has a clothes-optional area on the far side. The hotel operates a water taxi service.

Dominican Republic

Eden Bay

Playa Grande, Abreu, Cabrera
A dedicated all-inclusive nude resort set in a beautiful natural bay with the Caribbean ocean lapping on the bare beach. White sand, palm trees and lush vegetation all conspire to make this tropical holiday resort a must for all-over tan enthusiasts.

Hotel La Plantation
www.la-plantation.com
hotel@la-plantation.com
Tel: 00 590 29 58 00
Fax: 00 590 29 58 08
Vacations.net

Cap Caraibes Hotel
www.cap-caraibes.com
capcaraibes@wanadoo.fr
Tel: 00 590 52 94 94
Fax: 00 590 52 95 00
Hoteldiscount.com

Caribbean Nature
membres.lycos.fr/naturissimo/
membres.lycos.fr/legalion/
naturismenature@wanadoo.fr
Book direct

Wyndham El Conquistador
www.wyndham.com/resorts/sjuec/
pvp@wyndham.com
Tel: 00 1 787 863 1000
Fax: 00 1 787 863 6586
Interhotel.com

Eden Bay
www.edenbay.com
edenbay@codetel.net.do
edenbayresort@aol.com
Tel: 00 1 809 589 7750
Castaways Travel (USA)

Club Med Turquoise
www.clubmed.co.uk
lonbmktg01@clubmed.com
Tel: 00 1 649 946 55 00
Fax: 00 1 649 946 54 97
Club Med UK

Turks and Caicos Islands

Bare beach close to Club Med Turquoise

Providenciales

This is a lovely quiet nude beach with **fine white sand** slipping into an azure sea, ideal for swimming and snorkelling.

The bare beach is signposted and is just 5 minutes' walk along the shore from the nearby adult **Club Med** resort.

Bahamas

Eleuthera bare beaches

Eleuthera island, 30 minutes local flight from Nassau

Set apart on its own pink beach, **Sable Rose**, right, is the very peak of romantic bare bathing heaven

Two **deserted bare beaches** to die for. Soft pink sand and translucent sea must make this pair high-ranking on any 'world's best' listing – and they are perfect for indulging yourself as nature intended. Add to that, just **one luxury holiday house on each beach** and you know you're on to something special. You can fly direct to Nassau from London Heathrow by British Airways.

Aarons Beachhouse, 7 miles north of the island capital, Governor's Harbour, is built in a contemporary style and has two bedrooms and two bathrooms, while **Sable Rose** located near North Palmetto Point sleeps just two people. Booking enquiries should be made with the bare-friendly owner, John Bennett, by email.

Aarons Beachhouse and **Sable Rose**
www.bahamas-beach-rental.com
jb33139@aol.com
Book direct

Cuba

Cayo Largo bare beaches

An island in the Los Canarreos archipelago, south-east from the capital Havana

Here you will find all the ingredients of a tropical **garden of Eden** – great expanses of white sand as fine as talcum powder, warm clear turquoise sea and almost permanent sunshine. Just 25 miles long, the island has lots of **completely undeveloped beaches**. Bare bathing, which has a long tradition here, is widely practised and accepted. There is a cluster of all-inclusive properties forming the **Gran Caribe Resort**. A

Cayo Largo holidays
www.grancaribe.cu
www.cayolargodelsur.cu
www.captivating-holidays.com/cuba
isla@isla.gca.cma.net or
sales@gran-caribe.com
Tel: 00 537 204 6366 or
020 8959 3700 (London)
Fax: 00 537 204 4181
or 020 8906 8862 (London)
Captivating Cuba (UK),
Gran Caribe Group

favourite with cabana style rooms, close to a pleasant nude beach, is **Hotel Villa Lindamar** (for details see www.cayolargodelsur.cu).

Lily and Normand from Canada have developed an excellent website about the island and its au naturel opportunities: see www.cayolargo.net

Honduras

Paya Bay bare beach

On the north-eastern shore of Roatan, Bay Islands

There are two lovely beaches at this resort, the smaller of which is perfect for bare bathing. According to the management, 'it is clothes-optional for the use of our guests, very secluded and private'.

Just 100 metres offshore lies the **Mayan Barrier Reef**, said to be the **second largest in the world** – obviously a very popular choice for divers. The **Paya Bay** all-inclusive beach and dive resort has attractive cabins overlooking the Caribbean.

Paya Bay resort
www.payabay.com
payabay@globalnet.hn
Tel: 00 504 435 2139 or
00 1 936 628 2204 (US office)
Fax: 00 504 435 2149 or
00 1 936 628 6081 (US office)
Book direct or through US
Reservations Office

Tropical Eden: **Cayo Largo**'s Hotel Barcelo beach, eastern end. Picture courtesy www.cayolargo.net

The Americas

Mix the friendly atmosphere of a nudist holiday resort with the American service culture and you know you're on to a winner.

The au naturel lifestyle is well established in North America and large sums of money have been poured into developing inland nudist resorts and clubs. It is estimated that travellers taking holidays in the buff are spending more than $400 million each year, and the figure keeps growing.

The US has a long and mostly beautiful coastline with a number of well-used bare beaches. Not as many as in Europe, but there are some well established and popular nude sea-bathing places. We have listed some of the best.

Canada, with its French connection, has a more relaxed attitude to bare bodies and there are some hugely popular, world-class nude beaches to satisfy demand. And Brazil, the place famed for its beach life, has started to shed what little remains of its swimwear. A bare beach in Rio de Janeiro was given full legal blessing in November 2003.

Mexico

Hidden Beach

Kantenah Bay, Tulum

The beaches on the **Caribbean coast** of Mexico mostly consist of dazzling white sand lapped by deep blue sea. The shore in front of the new clothes-optional **boutique resort** of **Hidden Beach** is no exception, making it ideal for au naturel relaxation.

Underwater rocks mean care is needed entering the sea, but the resort has an **attractive pool** for skinny dipping right next to the beach.

The property, which opened in 2003, has **42 luxury suites** all facing the sea. Accommodation on the ground floor has a clever 'swim-up' river that connects to the main swimming pool so you don't even need to walk to the swim-up bar.

Guests at the resort can also use the facilities of the larger **Eldorado clothed resort** next door, which is owned by the same company.

Hidden Beach resort
www.hiddenbeachresort.com
sales@hiddenbeachresort.com
Canarian Dreams, Castaways
Travel (USA)

A heavenly way to de-stress – and that's just the bare beach. **Hidden Beach resort** is long on luxury. Pictures supplied by resort

Caribbean Reef Club
www.caribbeanreefclub.com

Rancho Libertad
www.rancholibertad.com

Diamante-K Ecological Hotel
www.diamantek.com

Cabanas Copal Hotel
www.cabanascopal.com

Maya Tulum Retreat
www.mayatulum.com

Playa Naturel
www.playanaturel.com

Tankah Villa and Cabanas
www.sliceofparadise.com

Playa Sonrisa
www.playasonrisa.com

Haulover beach, in Florida, is fine for winter sunshine and summer chilling – and it's easy to reach

Other bare beaches in Mexico

There are plenty of other informal places to stay on Mexico's Caribbean coast that provide opportunities for bare bathing and relaxation. All the resorts and accommodation listed here are handy for naked sunseekers. The **Caribbean Reef Club**, at Puerto Morelos, near Cancun, has a bare beach, pool and hot tub. **Rancho Libertad**, Puerto Morelos, has a bare beach area, and **Diamante-K Ecological Hotel**, Tulum, is next to a nude beach.

Cabanas Copal Hotel, Tulum, is a clothes-optional holistic spa which also has a bare beach. Also in Tulum, **Maya Tulum Retreat** has an au naturel beach. **Playa Naturel**, at Tankah Beach, Xel-ha, near Tulum, is a yoga and health spa with a small naturist beach.

Tankah Villa and Cabanas, at Tankah near Tulum, has a secluded clothes-optional beach, and **Playa Sonrisa**, at Xcalak, on Costa Maya, also has a bare beach.

The United States

Florida

Haulover beach

Sunny Isles, North Miami
Situated in the south of the 'Sunshine State', this **officially bare sandy beach** set in the regional park has a huge following of regular visitors from across the globe. With glorious weather for most of the year and the **vibrant city of Miami** on the doorstep, it's not difficult to see why so many people love chilling out at Haulover.

The bare area is more than 800 yards long and has its own **lifeguard lookout** posts. Refreshments are on sale, and sunbeds and umbrellas are available to hire. Toilets are located directly behind the beach. The **cosmopolitan crowd** here often hold impromptu barbecues and at weekends there's a particularly lively atmosphere. The bare area is clearly marked and signposted and regular but

unobtrusive police patrols ensure the beach is **well managed, safe and secure**.

The South Florida Free Beaches Association estimates well over **half a million undressed holidaymakers** enjoy sunning and swimming here every year. They promote the beach as **family-friendly** and have an informative website with location maps and hotels: www.sffb.com

It is easy to find the beach, which is at **Haulover Beach Miami-Dade** county regional park, on Collins Avenue (A1A), just north of fashionable **Bal Harbour**. There is a large car park ($4) with a pedestrian tunnel under the main road leading straight to the bare beach. Alternatively, use the Metrobus to get to the park and the beach.

While there is a good selection of all grades of hotel in the general vicinity, there are two simple **beachside motels** offering basic rooms within a 250-yard stroll of the nude area. **Ocean Palm Motel** is nearest the bare beach and the **Days Inn Hotel** is next door to it.

Ocean Palm Motel
Tel: 00 1 305 947 5671
Book direct

Days Inn Hotel
www.daysinn.com
Tel: 00 1 305 940 0237
Fax: 00 1 305 940 1211
Book direct or through Daysinn.com

California

Black's beach and San Onofre beach

San Diego County, southern California
Two established but remote bare beaches on the Pacific surfing coast, south of **Los Angeles**. Both have attractive natural biscuit-coloured sandy shorelines with backdrops of undeveloped hills and cliffs. Although **Black's beach** is probably better known, it requires a steep **300-foot climb down** on a way-marked path and, more importantly, another climb up again at the end of the day to reach the car park.

San Onofre is to the north of Black's beach and has **easier access** from the low hills behind the coast. **Dolphins and seals** are often seen basking near both locations. Traditional nude use of the beaches has ensured they are well used by locals and holidaymakers alike.

Black's beach is immediately west of the University of California's **San Diego Campus**. Take Interstate 5 to **La Jolla** and follow signs to the **Torrey Pines Scenic Drive**. From there take the paved track (which turns into a dirt track) to the Glider Port and park. A steep path to the south leads down to the beach – wear sensible shoes or boots.

San Onofre state beach is reached by taking Interstate 5 to the **Basline Road** exit. Go past the nuclear power plant and into the state park ($3). Drive 3 miles and park at Trail 6, at the end of the track (toilets – restroom 16). Take the path down to the beach and walk 600 yards south to the bare area, just past the life guard station. Bare beach information is available from wanr.earthbiz.net

Golden Gate Baker Beach

Presidio, San Francisco
An iconic bare beach at the foot of rugged cliffs with the famous **Golden Gate bridge** as a backdrop. For a long time San Francisco has had a laid-back approach to beach nudity, enabling the city's residents to enjoy their relaxation in the buff. There are fantastic views, but strong currents make the sea **hazardous for swimming**.

Located between **Sea-Cliff** and the **Golden Gate Bridge**. From downtown, drive west on Geary and then north on 25th Avenue then turn right on to **Presidio**. The car park is on **Gibson Road** – use the furthest east spaces. It is a five-minute walk along the shore to the clothing-optional area.

New York

Lighthouse beach

Fire Island, Long Island
A wonderfully unspoilt and spacious sandy beach, which is easy to get to. The shore is well managed by rangers with a reputation for being friendly and **supportive towards bare bathers** and sunseekers. Not surprisingly the beach is popular and attracts all age groups including a significant number of families. It's certainly an excellent antidote to the hurly burly of New York city

A **boardwalk across the dunes** from the car park facilitates disabled access. There are separate clothes-optional areas on either side of the boardwalk – the one to the west extends for half a mile and tends to **attract more visitors** and the one to the east stretches for two-thirds of a mile and is usually less busy.

You are expected to walk 150 yards beyond the access, in either direction, before undressing. There is plenty of space for strolling in the buff along the water's edge, but if you go swimming beware: in certain conditions there is a **strong undertow**. Take refreshments and a picnic with you.

Drive on to **Long Island**, take the Robert Moses Parkway (south) and follow it directly to the beach. Head for Parking Lot 5, which is well signed. You have to pay a charge to park here. Walk to the east of the bathhouse, on the **lighthouse** side, and keep walking until you see the prominent sign announcing the clothing-optional beach.

Hawaii

Little beach

Makena State Park, southern coast of Maui
Another world famous bare beach that attracts swimmers, snorkellers, surfers and sunseekers. A **romantic and secluded cove**, particularly popular with young people and which regularly features in lists of best nude beaches – and not only American ones. A **bare wedding** here recently featured on the Travel Channel.

Backed by low cliffs and pine trees, the Pacific ocean rolls up on the soft golden sand. Normally plenty of space for everybody but bring your own shade and refreshments. An **unusual phenomenon** in winter – during stormy weather much of the sand can be washed completely away one day, and then return again the next.

A useful website for up-to-date information on the beach is www.littlebeachmaui.com

Drive south on Route 31, past **Wailea Golf** and follow signs to **Makena La Perouse state park**. Pass the Maui Prince Hotel en route. Go as far north as possible to park and walk on to 'Big beach'. Turn right and continue north to the end of the beach, taking the easy lava flow trail over the narrow headland to Little beach – it's not a difficult journey.

A local agent – Donna Stafford of **Chameleon Vacation Rentals** – has lots of good quality holiday accommodation on the island, and can provide advice on a range of clothing-optional and nude-friendly places to stay on Maui, including some near to Little beach. Among these are **Polly Makena Beachfront Villas** – at Makena, Ahihi Bay, South Shore. These two luxurious Polynesian pole-style villas on the shore at Ahihi Bay are described as clothes-optional. Little beach is a five-minute drive or a pleasant 30-45 minute walk along Big beach.

Maui House Kihei Cottage is at Maui Meadows, Kihei, South Shore. A quality one-bedroom holiday home set in lush gardens a mile from the coast, the property is clothing-optional and there is a chlorine-free swimming pool and spa pool. Little beach is a 10-minute drive from the property.

Chameleon Vacation Rentals
www.donnachameleon.com
info@donnachameleon.com
Tel: 00 1 866 575 9933 (toll free)
Fax: 00 1 801 340 8537

Brazil

Abricó bare beach

Recreio dos Bandeirantes (south zone), Rio de Janeiro
A **gorgeous, secluded white sand** bare beach on the outskirts of this exciting city. After many requests from locals, the authorities recently agreed to grant **official nude status** to this idyllic little bay, which has an unspoilt backdrop of natural green vegetation.

Now we are nude: the city with the world's smallest swimming costumes has bowed to the inevitable and given bare beach lovers a place of their own. **Abricó beach**, below, already has its loyal users after finally going bare in November 2003

As an alternative to the sand, smooth rocks at the side of the beach provide a sunbathing platform just above the ocean. There is already a **thriving beach community** and the locals have an informative website (in Spanish) with lots of photographs and other info: www.abrico.cjb.net

The bare cove borders the clean, and isolated **Grumari beach** on the edge of the city.

Canada

Wreck beach

Vancouver, British Columbia
This is a beautifully wild beach with pine woods coming right down to the sand. This officially clothing-optional shoreline stretching for 6 kms is well known in nudist circles, and on sunny weekends attracts **thousands of visitors**.

The forested cliffs rise to 200 feet above where the Fraser River joins the Strait of Georgia. The beach is also an **ornithologist's paradise** with eagles, kingfishers, local Great Blue herons, pileatted woodpeckers and even domestic birds such as parrots, lovebirds and magpies.

To get to this much-loved spot, drive or take the bus to south-west **Marine Drive** on the western edge of the city, by the University of British Columbia Campus. Park at **Trail 6** and follow the path down to the main bare beach.

Bare beach information from: www.wreckbeach.org

Hanlan's Point beach

Toronto Island, Ontario

This lovely bare beach is maintained by the City of Toronto's parks department and has **lifeguards and other facilities**. It was only granted official nude status in 1999 and now has a dedicated following of all-over tan seekers.

Catch the ferry over to **Hanlan's Point** from the terminal at the foot of Bay Street. Walk along the paved path past the airport and continue until you are at the beach (5-10 minutes). Once on the beach, walk away from the airport (south) until you get to the bare area.

If in doubt, simply look for the signs that identify the clothing-optional section.

Wreck beach in Canada, below, is one of the Travel Channel's top 10 nude beaches. It's made a lot of people very content and very brown over the years, and has a thriving, colourful community

Africa

So who invented bare bathing? Europe's naturist pioneers of the early 20th century certainly did much to promote it, but in truth they simply reintroduced what everyone always used to do. Until the swimming costume was foisted on the world by the red-faced Victorians, the idea of getting dressed to go swimming hadn't occurred to most people.

There are plenty of places where people have bathed naked since time began, and continue to do so.

And while Africa has had its fair share of interference, there are still many places where ideas such as naturism wouldn't mean anything. It's just called going swimming.

These aren't destinations for bare bathing tourists as such, although there's plenty of wilderness and desert to explore in southern Africa. And if you want to add a beautiful bare beach to your itinerary, Cape Town is the place to go.

Swimming as they always have, children play in the village of Dembel Jumpora, Guinea-Bissau (top right), picture courtesy Ami Vitale.
Sandy Bay (bottom right) has long been a favourite of Cape Town's local and tourist bare bathers alike. Picture courtesy Villa Antoinette B&B

Sandy Bay, South Africa

Llandudno, Cape Town

Sandy Bay is a much-loved haven for nude bathers in South Africa. It's been accepted as a nude beach for decades, sitting as it does in **peaceful isolation** 20 minutes' walk from the nearest parking. Needless to say it's a sandy beach, but with **rocky coves to explore**. It's not protected if the Cape south-east winds blow. It's a beautiful place, well worth the 1.5 mile walk from the car parking.

To get here drive along the coast road that winds round **Table Mountain** to the little **suburb of Llandudno**. Parking here is limited, so arrive early or you'll have a longer walk. Take the coastal path down to the bay.

And if you want a welcoming place to stay, **Villa Antoinette B&B** in the City Bowl at a place called **Verdehoek** is just 20 minutes' drive away. It has two en-suite bedrooms and spectacular views of Table Mountain from the secluded terrace. The owners Hans and Denise are naturists, and can help give directions to Sandy Bay. The accommodation itself is not naturist – unless all the guests want it to be.

Cape Town
city centre

Sandy
Bay   Llandudno

Villa Antoinette B&B
www.villa-antoinette.co.za
villaantoinette@iafrica.com
Tel/fax: 00 27 21 465 9623
Book direct with the owners Hans and Denise

Bare facts

Bare-friendly travel agents in the UK

The companies listed here actively promote holidays where you can get an all-over tan. They can advise on bare beaches and bare sunbathing areas at hotels, with the latest information on suitable facilities. Remember that bare bathing opportunities can change so it's worth checking when you book. The main British travel agents also offer resorts with or near bare bathing places but it's not a priority for them so they are less likely to have current details.

Peng Travel
A member of ABTA that has sold naturist holidays in the UK for 30 years.
Tel: 0845 345 8345
www.pengtravel.co.uk

France 4 Naturisme
A range of holidays at French naturist resorts
Tel: 01797 364315 (Suzanne Piper)
www.france4naturisme.com

Canarian Dreams International
Bare beach holidays in the Canaries and the Caribbean
Tel: 0870 770 5378
www.canariandreams.com

Chalfont Holidays
European naturist holidays in a choice of resorts
Tel: 01494 580728
www.chalfontholidays.co.uk

Island Seekers
Holidays on Lanzarote and Fuerteventura for bare bathers
Tel: 0870 112 0555
www.islandseekers.co.uk

Sunseekers
Wide range of quality self-catering properties on Fuerteventura
Tel: 08700 660 480
www.sunseekerholidays.com

Don't blush!
These travel agents make their money from bare beach holidays, and expect their customers to want an all-over tan. But if you're speaking to a non-nude travel agent you can always try asking for a room with a sunny balcony that isn't overlooked

Astbury Formentera
Specialises in self-catering apartments on Formentera in
the Balearics
Tel: 01642 210163
formentera.co.uk

It's Natural
Self-catering naturist accommodation at Vera Playa, Almeria,
south-east Spain
Tel: 01354 661511
www.its-natural.net

Away with Dune
Worldwide naturist and bare beach holidays, specialises in
escorted trips to Crete
Tel: 0870 751 8866
www.dune.uk.com

AV Travel
Naturist-friendly holidays to France, the Canaries and
the Caribbean
Tel: 01305 767777
www.avtravel.co.uk

Hunter Travel
UK agent for Costa Natura naturist resort, Spain
Tel: 01256 761977
www.huntertravel.co.uk

Travellers' Way
Rural hotels and apartments in the Canaries with advice on
bare bathing
Tel: 01527 559000
www.travellersway.co.uk

Club Holidays
Naturist mobile-home holidays in the South of France
Tel: 01604 863300
www.clubholidays.net

Bare-friendly travel agents in the US

Internaturally Travel
US-based company for nudist holidays and resorts, also publishers of a quarterly naturist travel magazine – see website for details
Tel: 00 1 973 697 8099
www.internaturally.com

Castaways Travel
US-based company offering clothes-optional holidays and cruises
Tel: 00 1 281 362 8785
www.castawaystravel.com

Bare Necessities
US based, specialising in clothes-optional chartered cruise liners
Tel: 00 1 512 499 0405
www.bare-necessities.com

Fantastic Voyages
US based, with a division specialising in clothes-optional resorts
Tel: 00 1 817 568 8611
www.fantasticvoyages.com

All-Inclusive Travel Inc
US internet company with a clothes-optional division
Tel: 00 1 954 979 1970
www.bareaffair.net

Go Classy Tours
US-based tour operator with clothes-optional holiday division
Tel: 00 1 727 781 1405
www.gonude.com

Travel Au Naturel
US-based company for clothes-optional cruises and resorts
Tel: 00 1 813 948 2007
www.travelaunaturel.com

Au Naturel Travel
www.aunaturelvacations.com

Bare bathing on cruise ships

Cruise Ship AIDA

Mediterranean in summer / Caribbean in winter
A modern luxury 1200-berth cruise liner, recently acquired by the P&O Group. The ship caters mainly for the German market and operates from Palma, Majorca, in the summer and from Santa Domingo, in the Dominican Republic, in the winter. It has a permanent 'FKK deck' reserved for nude sunbathing at the stern on deck 10, on the port side.

Cruise Ship Oriana (and others in the fleet)

A luxury P&O cruise liner with 914 cabins, of which 118 have private balconies. Recent full-page advertisements placed by the company in the UK press showed a naked sunbather and read: 'White bits, what white bits? A cabin with a sun-baked private balcony certainly adds a whole new dimension to your holiday. On your private balcony, you can watch the world go by, not vice-versa.'

Chartered clothes-optional cruises

Naturist travel companies in America are chartering an increasing number of large luxury liners for nude Caribbean cruises. They normally depart from Miami, Florida throughout the year. Holidays are offered by Travel Au Naturel, Castaways Travel, Bare Necessities, Go Classy Tours and Fantastic Voyages. All contact details on page opposite.

Cruise ship AIDA
www.aida.de
info@aida.de
P&O Cruises

Oriana and others
www.pocruises.com
Tel: 020 7800 2222
Fax: 020 7831 1410
P&O Cruises

Fully naturist holiday resorts

Everyone should try skinny-dipping. If you love it so much you want more, there's a whole world of naked holidays waiting for you (see page 44).

France
- Club Oasis, Port Leucate
  www.oasis-village.com
- Aphrodite Village, Port Leucate
  www.aphrodite-village.org
- Cap d'Agde, Agde
  www.capdagde.co.uk
- Arnaoutchot, Vielle-St-Girons
  www.arna.com
- La Jenny, Le Porge
  www.lajenny.fr
- Montalivet, Montalivet
  www.chm-montalivet.com
- Euronat, Montalivet
  www.euronat.fr
- Cap Natur, St Hilaire de Riez
  www.cap-natur.com
- Belezy, Bedoin
  www.belezy.com
- Sabliere, Barjac
  www.campingsabliere.com
- Club Origan, nr Nice
  www.club-origan.com
- Riva Bella, Corsica
  www.rivabella-corsica.com
- Piana Verde, Corsica
  www.pianaverde.com
- La Chiappa, Corsica
  www.chiappa.com

Spain
- Costa Natura, Estepona
  www.costanatura.com
- Vera Natura, Vera Playa
  www.veranatura.com
- Bahia de Vera, Vera Playa
  www.marenostrumsa.com

Pay and display
The only difference between most naturist resorts and an ordinary resort is the freedom to leave your cossie in the suitcase. A few places expect you to have a naturist membership card (see page 198), but even then they're likely to just issue one at reception. At some places you can just turn up, although like any holiday site booking is always advised, especially in high season

- Natsun, Vera Playa
  www.natsun.com
- Parque Vera, Vera Playa
  www.veraplaya.info
- El Portus, Cartagena
  www.elportus.com
- La Jaquita, Tenerife
  www.teneriffa-urlaub.de

Holland

- Flevo-Natuur, Flevoland
  www.flevonatuur.nl

Croatia

- Valalta, Rovinj
  www.valalta.hr
- Monsena, Rovinj
  www.monsena.com
- Koversada, Porec/Rovinj
  www.koversada.com
- Solaris, Porec
  www.istra.com/porec/eng/fkk.html

Caribbean

- Club Orient, St Martin
  www.cluborient.com
- Sorobon Beach, Bonaire
  www.sorobonbeachresort.com
- Eden Bay, Dominican Republic
  www.edenbay.com

USA

- Cypress Cove, Kissimmee Fl
  www.suncove.com
- Paradise Lakes, Land O'Lakes Fl
  www.paradiselakes.com
- Caliente Resort, Land O'Lakes Fl
  www.calienteresort.com
- Desert Shadows, Palm Springs Ca
  www.desertshadows.com
- Terra Cotta, Palm Springs Ca
  www.sunnyfun.com

British Naturism
30-32 Wycliffe Road
Northampton
NN1 5JF
Tel: 01604 620361
Fax: 01604 230176
www.british-naturism.org.uk

International Naturist Federation
www.inffni.org

Naturist UK FactFile
www.nuff.org.uk

H&E Naturist
www.healthandefficiency.co.uk
Tel: 01405 764206

The Naturist Society
www.naturist.com

Naturist Life
www.shabden.co.uk
Tel: 01797 364315

Sources of naturist information

British Naturism

The Central Council for British Naturism, more commonly referred to as British Naturism, is the national body for organised naturism in the UK. It aims to further the acceptance of naturist leisure in Britain and offers membership for interested individuals. A quarterly magazine, including holiday advice and a huge range of advertising, is sent to members. The website also has details of UK bare beaches and includes an extensive list of links to overseas holiday resorts and foreign naturist organisations.

International Naturist Federation

The INF brings together all national naturist organisations from around the world, including British Naturism. It publishes a World Handbook of naturist clubs and resorts every two years. Individual members of British Naturism are automatically members of this international body of naturists, and receive a membership card accordingly. Some of the fully naturist resorts listed in this section might require a naturist membership card, particularly in France, but a temporary local membership can normally be purchased on arrival if needed.

Naturist UK FactFile

NUFF is an internet resource operated by a group of enthusiasts committed to broadening the range of information freely available to those seeking details of British naturist activities and venues. It also includes overseas trip reports.

H&E Naturist

This retail magazine is published monthly in the UK. 'Health & Efficiency' has a long and venerable history stretching back over more than 100 years of continuous publication. Today it contains up to the minute editorial and features aiming to provide a modern guide for enthusiasts about naturist living and holidays.

The Naturist Society

A US-based organisation that promotes naturist recreation and also produces the well-researched Nude & Natural magazine.

Naturist Life

This UK-based naturist magazine is published by Shabden Leisure Circle, a naturist club. It has plenty of travel features.

UK airlines/national tourist boards

Big four low-cost airlines

easyJet	www.easyjet.com
Ryanair	www.ryanair.com
bmibaby	www.bmibaby.com
flybe	www.flybe.com

Other UK low-cost airlines

duo	www.duo.com
FlyGlobespan	www.flyglobespan.com
jet2	www.jet2.com
Monarch	www.flymonarch.com
Mytravelite	www.mytravelite.com
Thomsonfly	www.thomsonfly.com

For complete low-cost airline information, www.cheap0.com is a single source of information on more than 1,250 no-frills routes right across the continent.

Full service airlines

British Airways	www.ba.com
BMI	www.bmi.com
Virgin Atlantic	www.virgin-atlantic.com

Main charter airlines

Thomson Flights	www.thomson.co.uk
Mytravel Flights	www.uk.mytravel.com
First Choice Flights	www.air2000.com
Thomas Cook Flights	www.thomascook.co.uk

Official tourist boards

France	www.tourisme.fr
(plus naturist info at)	uk.franceguide.com
Spain	www.tourspain.co.uk
Greece	www.gnto.gr
Croatia	www.croatia.hr
Portugal	www.portugal.org
Australia	www.australia.com
New Zealand	www.purenz.com
Bahamas	www.bahamas.com
Mexico	www.visitmexico.com
Florida	www.flausa.com
California	www.visitcalifornia.com
South Africa	www.southafrica.net

Aeroscope Holidays	www.aeroscope.co.uk	01608 650103
Agroturismo Balear (Mallorca)	www.baleares.com/fincas	00 34 971 71 71 22
Airglobe Holidays	www.airglobe.com	0870 708 5666
Airtours	www.airtours.com	0870 238 7788
Amathus	www.amathusholidays.co.uk	0870 443 2972
Argo	www.argo-holidays.com	0870 066 7070
Astbury Formentera	www.formentera.co.uk	01642 210163
AV Travel	www.avtravel.co.uk	01305 767777
Away with Dune	www.dune.uk.com	0870 751 8866
Balkan Holidays	www.balkanholidays.co.uk	0845 130 1114
Bosmere Travel	www.bosmeretravel.co.uk	01473 834094
Cadogan	www.cadoganholidays.com	023 80828300
Canarian Dreams/Caribbean Dreams	www.canariandreams.com	0870 770 5378
Captivating Croatia	www.captivating-holidays.com	0870 887 0124
Caribbean Expressions	www.expressionsholidays.co.uk	020 7431 2131
Caribtours	www.caribtours.co.uk	020 7751 0660
Castaways (UK)	www.castaways.co.uk	01737 812255
Chalfont Holidays	www.chalfontholidays.co.uk	01494 580728
Classic Collections	www.classic-collection.co.uk	0870 787 3377
Club Holidays	www.clubholidays.net	01604 863300
Corona	www.coronahols.com	020 8530 2500
Cosmos	www.cosmos-holidays.co.uk	0870 44 35 285
Davimar Tours (Mallorca)	www.davimar.com	00 34 971717122
Direct Holidays	www.directholidays.co.uk	0870 238 7700
Eclipse	www.eclipseholidays.com	0870 243 4300
Elegant Resorts	www.elegantresorts.co.uk	01244 897 000
Falcon Holidays	www.falconholidays.co.uk	028 90 389 387
First Choice	www.firstchoice.co.uk	0870 850 3999
France 4 Naturisme	www.france4naturisme.com	01797 364315
Funway	www.funwayholidays.co.uk	0870 22 00 626
Hallmark	www.worldchoiceweb.co.uk/hallmark	01702 710333
Hayes & Jarvis	www.hayesandjarvis.co.uk	0870 89 89 890
Holiday Hotels	www.holidayhotels.co.uk	0870 2731273
Holiday Options	www.holidayoptions.co.uk	0870 420 8386
Inghams	www.inghams.co.uk	020 8780 4400
Island Seekers	www.islandseekers.co.uk	0870 112 0555
JMC	www.jmc.com	0870 750 5711
Kompas d.d. (Croatia)	www.kompas.hr	00 385 1 48 78 750
Kosmar Holidays	www.kosmar.co.uk	0870 7000 747
Kuoni	www.kuoni.co.uk	01306 747002
Libra	www.libraholidays.co.uk	0871 226 0446
Millennium & Copthorne Hotels	www.millenniumhotels.com	020 7872 2444
Mundi Color	www.mundicolor.co.uk	020 7828 6021
Olympic	www.olympicholidays.co.uk	0870 429 4141
Orchid Travel	www.orchid-travel.com	0870 757 0370
Panorama	www.panoramaholidays.co.uk	0870 238 7744
Peng Travel	www.pengtravel.co.uk	0845 345 8345
Portland	www.portland-holidays.co.uk	0870 241 3172
Prestige Holidays	www.prestigeholidays.com	0700 392 2222
Real Spain	www.citalia.co.uk	020 8686 0677
Riviera Holidays (Croatia)	www.riviera.hr	00 385 52 451 379
Saga Holidays	www.saga.co.uk	0800 096 0074
Simply Greece	www.simplytravel.com	020 8541 2201
Sky Holidays	www.skyhols.com	0871 226 0449
Sovereign	www.sovereign.com	08703 661 634
Stein Travel (Ireland)	www.steintravel.ie	00 3531 408 6200
Sunseekers	www.sunseekerholidays.com	08700 660 480
Thomas Cook	www.thomascook.co.uk	0870 750 5711
Thomson	www.thomson.co.uk	0870 165 0079
Trailfinders	www.trailfinders.com	020 7938 3939
Transun	www.transun.co.uk	0870 4444 747
Travellers' Way	www.travellersway.co.uk	01527 559000
Unijet	www.unijet.com	0870 850 3999
Virgin	www.virginholidays.co.uk	0870 220 2788
Whitehall Leisure	www.whitehall-leisure.co.uk	020 7340 1030